Two Cities

TWO CITIES:
HANOI AND SAIGON

NEIL SHEEHAN

JONATHAN CAPE
LONDON

First published in Great Britain 1992
Jonathan Cape, 20 Vauxhall Bridge Road, London SW1V 2SA
© Neil Sheehan 1991, 1992

A portion of this work was originally published in different form as
'A Reporter at Large in Vietnam' in The New Yorker

Neil Sheehan has asserted his right under the Copyright, Designs and
Patents Act 1988 to be identified as the author of this work

A CIP catalogue record for this book
is available from the British Library

ISBN 0-224-03612-2

Printed in Australia by Griffin Paperbacks, Adelaide

For Robert Lescher
and for
Robert Loomis

Acknowledgments

As ever, I am in debt to my wife, Susan. Since I had the good fortune to meet her twenty-eight years ago, what I have done I have done with her help, or advice, or encouragement—usually with all three. This book is no exception. We collaborated on the reporting during our return to Vietnam and on the writing of an earlier, shorter version of the trip that appeared in *The New Yorker.* That article carried both of our bylines. I then decided to take the earlier magazine manuscript and my memories and turn them into this book of my own, and as always Susan talked me through the difficult moments and read and edited every draft.

I also wish to thank Robert Gottlieb, the editor of *The New Yorker,* for encouraging me to go back to Vietnam.

The quotations from Ho Chi Minh on pages 58–59 can be found in *War of the Vanquished* (New York: Harper & Row, 1971), by Mieczysław Maneli, the former senior Polish delegate to the International Commission for Supervision and Control created by the Geneva Agreements of 1954. Ambassador Maneli was an acquaintance during my first years in Vietnam in the early 1960s. His book is a brief but perceptive account of his experience there.

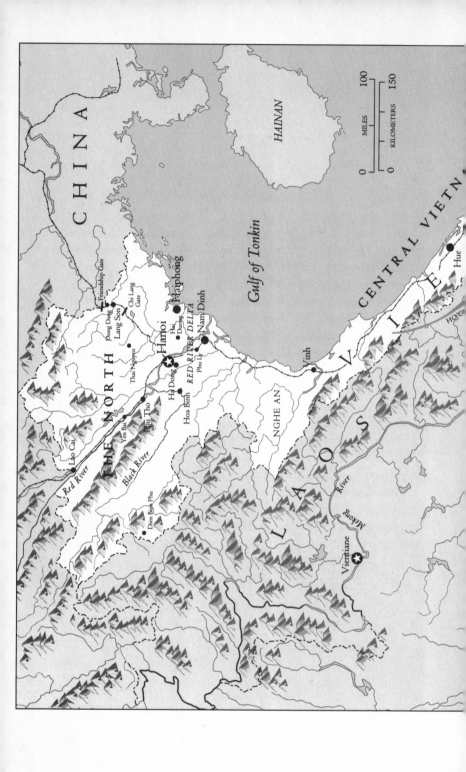

CHINA

HAINAN

MILES 0 100

KILOMETERS 0 150

Gulf of Tonkin

Friendship Gate
Dong Dang
Lang Son
Chi Lang Gate
Hai Duong
Haiphong

THE NORTH
Thai Nguyen
Hanoi
Ha Dong
RED RIVER DELTA
Nam Dinh
Phu Ly

Lao Cai
Yen Bai
Phu Tho
Hoa Binh

Red River
Black River

Dien Bien Phu

NGHE AN

Vinh

CENTRAL VIETNAM

Hue

LAOS

Mekong River

Vientiane

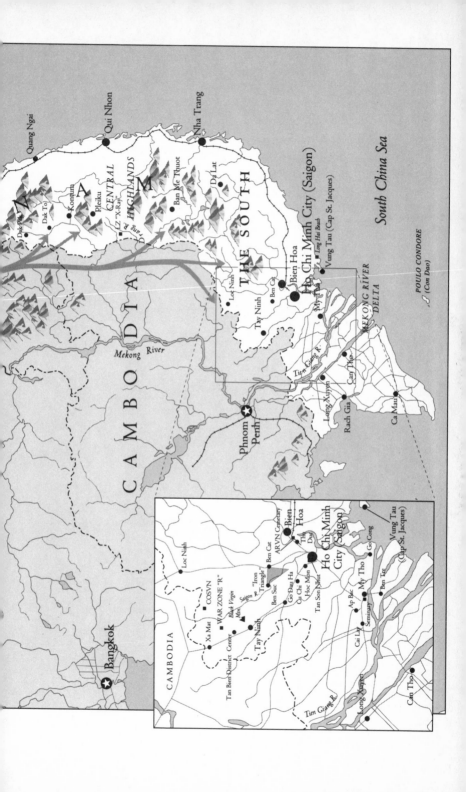

Hanoi
and the
North

Hanoi is a city caught in the warp of time, a place of history and icons, some dead, some still living to remind one that here the past never dies. Blank out the huge portrait of Ho Chi Minh on top of the National Bank building, the Banque de l'Indochine in its original incarnation, and one might be standing in a French colonial capital, a place of ornate ocher and white and other pastel-colored buildings erected to the glory of France at the turn of the century and in the 1920s and early '30s. Architecture in Hanoi essentially stopped in 1939 with the outbreak of World War II and the closing off of Indochina. The French reoccupied the city from 1946 to 1954, but during their vain attempt to reconquer their former colony they simply used what they had already built. As for the Vietnamese, they have been too busy and too impoverished fighting wars of independence against France and the United States and then a war in Cambodia and a border war with China to do much to change the face of their unique capital.

During my three years in Vietnam as a war correspondent in the 1960s I had told myself that one day I would return to the country when it was at peace, and finally, in the summer of 1989, the day came. My wife, Susan, and I arrived in Hanoi just as a typhoon was ending. I was accustomed to a Vietnamese capital in the flat expanse of the Mekong River delta because my Vietnam had been the South; Susan and I had lived in Saigon during the first year of our marriage twenty-four years earlier in the midst of the American war. As soon as the Thai Airways plane from Bangkok began to descend, I saw how different a place we were coming to this time. Here in the Red River delta of the North the foothills rise up to meet the inbound traveler. They march down from the mountains right to the edge of the plain. In the aftermath of the typhoon, the Red River was a swollen, curling flood from the torrents pouring into it out of the great watershed of mountains that ring this delta from China on the north all the way around past Laos on the west, the silt-laden flow more brown than red, despite the river's name. The rice paddies that extend out from both sides of the river were flooded too. Rain clouds still blew in from the South China Sea on the east, obscuring the paddies and the low-lying buildings.

The arrivals section of the terminal at Noi Bai Airport in the countryside north of the city was like a big, grubby shed. Dirt on the concrete floor crunched under the soles of one's shoes, the walls had wet stains from leaks and cracks from the settling of the foundation, and the place was rank with the odor of toilets. Most of the customs officers and immigration police were not wearing shoes or sneakers. They had rubber sandals on bare feet and were dressed in mismatched olive drab shirts and trousers—the shirt had apparently faded in the wash more than the trousers or vice versa. Several, including a woman customs supervisor who watched from a balcony, wore dark green army sun helmets, another item of clothing in frequent evidence in the North on military and civilians alike. The helmet, a plastic shell covered with cloth, was light and serviceable against both sun and rain. Everything else in view—the desks, the booths where the immigration officers sat to inspect and stamp passports—was just as forlorn from accumulated grime and want of paint. Tran Le Tien, one of the two guide-interpreters assigned to us by the Vietnamese Foreign Press Center, met us in a few minutes. I was glad to see him. The scene at Noi Bai, like other sights to come, was unsettling. It brought back the first of the questions echoing from the war: Why in the name of God had we bombed a country as poor as this?

The North had been forbidden territory during the war to those of us who covered the fighting in the South. We had wanted to go there out of a reporter's curiosity to see and describe this redoubt of the Communist "enemy," but the Vietnamese wouldn't let us come. They were too suspicious of reporters who knew something about the conflict. Having had no experience with a free press, they assumed that we, like most Soviet and Eastern European journalists, were members of an intelligence or propaganda service. Western journalists had occasionally been granted visas for circumscribed visits, including some distinguished American ones like Harrison Salisbury of *The New York Times*, who exposed the myth that the Pentagon was conducting a "surgical" bombing campaign against North Vietnam, but never reporters with extensive knowledge of the fighting in the South. The Vietnamese were afraid we might notice something we were not supposed to see, and they had reasoned, not always correctly, that the less familiar with the war, the more easily the reporter might be controlled.

The North we had seen through this prism of ignorance was the gray world of a small but spartan people marshaled under an authoritarian state, giving themselves single-mindedly to an unparalleled thirty-year endeavor to defeat first France and then the United States. What details we had in our heads we had gathered from the chroniclers of France's colonial disaster, from Jules Roy and his surpassingly eloquent account of the death of French dominion over this ancestral land of the Vietnamese in the shame and the valor of the battle of Dien Bien Phu, from Bernard Fall and his *Street Without Joy*, with its descriptions of the dance-on-the-doomed-deck ambiance of wartime Hanoi. The memory of Dien Bien Phu remained; the Vietnamese had celebrated the thirty-fifth anniversary of their victory that May. The ambiance was another matter, despite the time-capsule architecture of Hanoi, as we discovered when Tien took us to the hotel in the center of the city where most visiting journalists were put up, the famous Métropole of the French era, now called the Thong Nhat, which means "Reunification."

"The 'Hôtel Métropole' . . . was 'le dernier salon où l' on cause,' the last really fashionable place in Hanoi," Fall had written of his Hanoi of the 1950s. "Louis Blouet, its manager, had succeeded in exacting high standards of performance from his staff, which was as well-styled as that of his brother's 'Hôtel George V' in Paris and whose tipping scale was considerably lower than that of the Paris establishment. The headwaiter—a former colonel in the Chinese Nationalist forces—was as suave as his Paris counterpart and the barman could produce a reasonable facsimile of almost any civilized drink except water."

When I walked up the front steps of the hotel, past Grecian columns of peeling white paint, and pushed on the revolving door at the entrance, it turned grudgingly. The explanation was not in the heaviness of the once-handsome door: almost everything in Hanoi has been running down since 1939. The spindle on which the revolving door turned was worn out. Decades of guests coming and going, grinding grit underfoot, had also created dips in the marble of the entrance steps and the floor of the lobby. We went up to the room assigned to us on the third floor. It was large and held two old wooden beds with mosquito netting and a new Japanese refrigerator in an opposite corner. It was also redolent with years of mustiness, and, because I had stayed in rooms like it elsewhere in Asia during my young reportorial years, I could almost see the rats, even though I knew they probably would not come out until after dark. (An Australian friend stayed at the Thong Nhat with his son and daughter while we were in Hanoi. His son lost a large part of a sock to the rats one night, and his daughter was afraid to get out of bed to take a bath because the rats made so much noise gamboling about the room.) The room maid beckoned us into the bathroom with its museum-quality French plumbing and pointed up to a corner of the high ceiling. Dollops of rain leaking through the roof were kerplunking onto the tiles of the floor. (Later I wondered whether she had discouraged us further because she preferred having an empty room and thus no beds to make, or she was ashamed to have foreigners housed in such a place.)

I used Susan as an excuse to appeal to Tien's sense of gallantry. "My wife couldn't stand living in this hotel," I said. The Government Guest House, one of the few modern buildings in the central city, was a couple of blocks away. Once a genuine guest house where everything was free for officials and delegations from "friendly socialist countries," the place had become, in the days of change that were also overtaking Vietnam, a paying establishment where "honored foreign hard-currency guests" were preferred. The question of who could get in was still nebulous, but Tien talked the woman on the desk that day into giving us a room at one end of the second floor with an adjoining study where we could transcribe notes.

A three-story structure built in the mid-1970s right after the American war, the guest house was set in the back of a large garden compound behind the actual State Guest House, a colonial mansion that had been the residence of the French high commissioner for the region of the North and that was now reserved for genuine VIP visitors. Despite its more recent vintage, the place was hardly a Howard Johnson's motel. The air-conditioning units in the windows were 1970s models and rattled fearfully as if about to expire. This was not a pleasant prospect for sleeping since, as soon as the rain passed, the Hanoi summer temperature went back to the upper nineties, with extremely high humidity, moderating little at night. Yet after the frequent power failures the air conditioners always clattered back to life again. We kept flashlights on the bedside tables, and I carried one in my pocket on the streets at night. The staff was disorganized, trying to learn how to run a Western-style hotel (it was never clear precisely who the manager was), but they were friendly, kept the rooms clean, boiled the water so that it was safe to drink, and provided food that did not make one ill. There were rats, of course—rats are ubiquitous in Hanoi—but the Government Guest House rats confined themselves to the kitchen and the dining room.

Gen. Vo Nguyen Giap, the victor of Dien Bien Phu, was one of the living icons of Hanoi. He was not dressed in mismatching shirt and pants. The dark green of his short-sleeved uniform blouse, with red collar tabs bordered in gold and four gold stars on his shoulder insignia, matched his trousers perfectly, and both were elegantly cut. Giap was nearly seventy-eight years old in the summer of 1989, a bridge to history because he had been a companion of Ho Chi Minh, who had asked to be cremated and have his ashes scattered over Vietnam but had instead been preserved by his successors as an embalmed icon in a mausoleum that has become a national shrine.

The interview, in the reception room of the State Guest House, was supposed to be a formal one. The general brought a present of several branches of lichee fruit, which had just been given to him by a doctor who had served under him as a soldier at Dien Bien Phu. When Giap began by saying in French, "We'll chat," it seemed best to do just that and let this man tell who he was and where he was from rather than discuss yet again the few battles he had lost, the many he had won.

He spoke first of his boyhood in colonial times. He came from a provincial mandarin family, and his father, who had been educated in the Confucian classics, taught him how to read Vietnamese written in the pre-French way, in Chinese characters. He remembered sitting at home, cross-legged in Vietnamese fashion, reading about Ham Nghi, a heroic boy emperor whose mandarins had raised a major revolt against the French in the 1880s, and Duy Tan, the emperor who was deposed by the French in 1916 for plotting an insurrection among Vietnamese troops recruited for France's World War I battlefields. Giap's maternal grandfather had been the rebel commander of a province during Ham Nghi's revolt, and his mother talked to him of how the French troops had come to search for his grandfather. At night, before bedtime, his father would recite forbidden poems. Giap recalled one in particular. The poem was entitled "The Fall of Hue," about the French seizure of the imperial capital in 1883 and their sacking of it two years later during the Ham Nghi revolt. When Giap went to study at the lycée at Hue in 1925, his history textbook told him that what he had learned at home didn't matter. "Our country was called Gaul and our ancestors were the Gauls," Giap recited in a recollection from the French textbook. "When you think of the old days you never forget the shame of having lost your country," he said.

By 1940 he was twenty-nine years old, a history teacher at a lycée in Hanoi and a part-time journalist with a substantial police record for nationalist agitation and Communist Party activity. The French authorities launched a new campaign of repression after the outbreak of World War II, and he had to flee to China.. It was a Friday. The young woman who was Giap's first wife met him to say good-bye beside one of the lakes that dot the city. She brought their infant daughter with her. Giap didn't dare go home because he had to shake the police surveillance. He slept at a little hotel that night and the next morning slipped onto a train for the border town of Lao Cai, avoiding the Hanoi railway station and jumping on the train as it went across the bridge over the Red River. He did the same thing at the frontier, jumping off before Lao Cai and walking across the border into China. His wife, who was also a Party activist, was arrested by the French and died in prison during World War II. (Their infant daughter survived to become a nuclear physicist.) Giap did not return to Hanoi for five years. When he came back he was a scholar, a revolutionary, and an apprentice military leader. He commanded a fledgling Viet Minh guerrilla army that he had formed in the mountains below the Chinese border under the direction of Ho Chi Minh, the future president of Vietnam, who returned with him.

" 'You, professor of history, why did you become a soldier?' people ask me," Giap said, tilting his gray head back with a smile. "It was my destiny. It was natural for my whole generation." He laughed when I asked him if it was true that he never had any formal military training. Shortly before he left for China, a Party superior had told him that the time had come to begin an armed struggle. So he went to the main library in Hanoi, looked through an encyclopedia for things military, and found an article describing a grenade and read about how the grenade was set off by a detonator. "It was very difficult to understand." The encyclopedia entry on the grenade and his familiarity with a shotgun—the one firearm the colonial authorities permitted Vietnamese to own, for hunting—were "my sole knowledge in the matter of armaments," Giap said. The Japanese controlled Hanoi from March to August of 1945, when World War II ended. The Viet Minh then took over the city. After the French Army reoccupied Hanoi in 1946, Gen. Jacques Philippe Leclerc, who had liberated Paris from the Nazis, asked Giap what military school he had attended. Giap laughed once more as he relished his answer: "The military school of the jungle."

Giap continued, "You Americans didn't always come here to fight us." He recalled that when he and Ho Chi Minh first returned from the jungle in August 1945, a detachment from the U.S. Office of Strategic Services, the World War II forerunner of the Central Intelligence Agency, with which the Viet Minh had been collaborating against the Japanese, was already installed on the second floor of the Hôtel Métropole just out the front entrance and across the street from the former residence of the French high commissioner, where I was interviewing him. "You asked me if I had antipathy toward Americans," he remarked, referring to one of a list of written questions I had been required to submit before the meeting. Americans had once been his comrades in arms, Giap said. "How could I have antipathy toward Major Thomas?"—Maj. Allison Kent Thomas of the OSS. "He was with me at Thai Nguyen when we fought the Japanese."

The general pointed at the varnished doors leading to another room behind the chairs where we were sitting. He explained that while the OSS group was ensconced across the street in the hotel, "the president [he always referred to Ho by this title] and I were here in this building." The room behind us had been their office. He smiled and looked toward the floor above. The French high commissioner's bedroom up there had been their dormitory. "There was one big bed upstairs in which we all slept."

They hadn't been able to stay in Hanoi. The provocations of the returning French forced them into full-scale war in December 1946, and they retreated back into the mountains for another eight years of fighting until Dien Bien Phu put a coda to the first Vietnamese war for independence and brought them to Hanoi once more in triumph. "Voilà, history isn't a straight line, it's like a boulevard," Giap said. "From here to the jungle, then back here, then back to the jungle, then back here."

In 1982, despite the contribution he also made in the American war, Giap was forced out of the Politburo, the executive body of the Vietnamese Communist Party. He clashed with the late Le Duan, then general secretary of the Party, the Vietnamese Brezhnev, who is blamed for the economic mistakes and political dogmatism of the first decade after the defeat of the United States. Giap was shrewd enough not to retire from the army. He thus kept his villa in the best section of Hanoi, where the highest-ranking officials live, and he remained in public life, even though that meant the humiliation of standing behind the editor of the Party newspaper, Nhan Dan, on formal occasions when protocol ruled. One sensed there was a limit to how much such slights could hurt this man. He knew who he was and what he had done, and no one could take that away from him.

His current position, Vice-Premier for Science and Technology, was hardly a grand one; it did give him a role in the process of change that, amidst the icons, amidst the past that will continue to live, has been gaining momentum in Vietnam since the reformers got the upper hand at the Sixth Party Congress at the end of 1986. "Our country is like an ill person who has suffered for a long time," Giap said. "The countries around us made a lot of progress. We were at war." He spoke of the need for the Vietnamese to alter their way of thinking and to educate the young in science and technology if the country was to advance, but then he noted that this was not the first call for renewal of the Vietnamese nation and quoted a patriotic poem of his youth—"Each day anew, once more each day anew." The Vice-Premier for Science and Technology took his leave by kissing Susan on both cheeks in the manner of a courtly European gentleman of times gone by and then departed as a general of the army—down the steps at the front of the mansion to where his staff car, a black Soviet-made Volga sedan, was waiting on the driveway. He was followed into the car by his young aide and the rest of his entourage, including a doctor who was watching over him because he had a slight heart condition.

· · ·

The process of change that Giap spoke about is called *doi moi*, or "renovation," (literally, "new way"). The subject dominated almost every conversation because life in Vietnam was divided into what had happened before *doi moi* and what has happened since. "Drunk with victory" was the phrase Vietnamese used to describe the mind-set of their senior leadership during the decade after the fall of the U.S.-backed Saigon regime in 1975. The period is seen in retrospect as a time of tyranny and waste, a heedless attempt to create a visionary socialist state in defiance of reality, a folly that compounded the troubles inherited from the war and drove Vietnam into bankruptcy.

The Vietnamese would have had a bad time economically after the American war in any case. South Vietnam, when it existed as a separate entity from 1954 to 1975, was always an artificial society that lived off the United States. The former Saigon regime never earned more than a pittance from exports, but it imported hundreds of millions of dollars' worth of consumer products annually, all paid for by Washington. In addition, the United States shipped in millions of tons of free rice, and American military aid was a further source of income in the form of materials like gasoline that could be skimmed off and sold. Once the war began in earnest in 1965, the economy of the North too was sustained from the outside—by China, the Soviet Union, and the Eastern European countries—and the population willingly put up with rationing and shortages in order to win.

American aid to the South ceased overnight with the Communist victory in April 1975. The South had to go on existing without it. Yet much of the countryside in the South had been devastated; land had to be reclaimed and villages rebuilt. In addition, the war had created vast human problems: cities and towns with slums full of refugees; hundreds of thousands of unemployed former soldiers of the Saigon regime's army; an epidemic of heroin addiction that took years to quell.

The economic aid gap soon widened. With the American enemy vanquished, the historic animosity between Vietnam and China reasserted itself. The two governments quarreled seriously over

Chinese support for the Khmer Rouge regime of Pol Pot in Cambodia, and the Chinese suddenly cut off all of *their* aid in the spring of 1978. The aid gap then widened again. The Vietnamese were drawn into two more wars that further isolated them. At the end of 1978, unable to bear Pol Pot's attacks on their southern border any longer, the Vietnamese invaded Cambodia to over-throw him. China retaliated by launching an invasion of Vietnam's northern frontier. The United States thereupon joined China in organizing an economic boycott of Vietnam. Japan ceased its aid, as did most of the Western European countries. Under American pressure, the international lending institutions—the World Bank, the Asian Development Bank, the International Monetary Fund—denied Vietnam reconstruction loans.

The Vietnamese took note of these hardships imposed from outside and wished those still in force would cease, but they did not lay the principal blame for their economic troubles on them. They placed that blame on Le Duan, who was general secretary of the Party when Ho Chi Minh died in 1969. Le Duan inherited power, but not Ho's wisdom and flexibility, the Vietnamese said ruefully. With the country finally united after thirty years of war against the French and the Americans, Le Duan and his comrades of the old guard were determined to achieve the socialist state they had long dreamed of creating in an independent Vietnam. They were in a cocksure mood, not about to be deterred by the quarrel with China and the new wars Vietnam had to fight. After all, they had defeated the European colonizer and the greatest capitalist nation on earth.

Vietnam became a self-proclaimed "outpost of socialism in Southeast Asia." In the North agricultural land had already been collectivized into cooperatives where the peasants farmed in work brigades. In 1978 collectivization was extended to the farmland of the South and capitalism was virtually abolished throughout the country. All industry was nationalized and run on a rigidly central-ized basis by the State Planning Commission in Hanoi in imitation of the classic Communist economic model developed by Stalin in the Soviet Union during the 1930s. Factory managers were told what to make, how much to make, to whom they should sell their products, and what prices to charge. They were given raw materials at cheap, subsidized costs. (The raw materials were provided by the Soviet Union and the Eastern European countries, which had continued aid.) Soviet-made steel, for example, went to Vietnamese factories for the same price as duck eggs cost on the local market. Bigness and heavy industry were emphasized over the production of consumer goods. A factory manager's salary was based on how many workers he had, not on his factory's efficiency. All a manager had to do to succeed was to meet the annual production target. If his factory ran a deficit, the government picked up the tab by absorbing the debt. Happiness for all deserving citizens was the goal. (The motto of the Socialist Republic of Vietnam was, and is, "Independence, Liberty, Happiness.") No one was to go hungry, because everyone could go to a state store and purchase a monthly ration of rice at a low, government-subsidized price. Medical care at hospitals and clinics was free.

The rice subsidy alone was enormously expensive. One official estimated that it cost three times as much annually as the war in Cambodia. The state stores provided the monthly rice rations at 50 dong a kilogram, which had been the price of rice in North Vietnam in 1956. (A kilogram is equivalent to about 2.2 pounds.) Rice on the free market had meanwhile risen to ten times as much, 500 to 600 dong a kilogram. The government had to subsidize the difference but found it more difficult to obtain rice because production in the South fell after collectivization was extended there in 1978. The farmers had little incentive to produce; their share of the harvest had been reduced to about 20 percent. The other 80 percent went to the government in forced rice sales at less than market value—an attempt to hold down the cost of the subsidy—and to the "Red landlords," as the salaried bureaucrats who ran the cooperatives were derisively called by the peasantry. Natural disasters from typhoons and crop pests, particularly in Central Vietnam and the Red River delta, perennial rice-deficit areas, worsened the problem. The regime had to resort to spending precious hard currency to import rice from India and other Asian countries.

The machinery and other heavy-industry products Vietnamese factories did turn out were too old-fashioned or too shoddily made to sell abroad for hard currency with which to buy consumer goods. Soviet aid to Vietnam, worth about $2 billion annually during the 1980s (the aid ended in January 1991, almost a year before the demise of the Soviet state the following December), was not consumer oriented. A lot of it was military. The civilian assistance consisted mainly of materials for manufacturing, and materials and technical help for large-scale projects like hydroelectric stations. And since many of the Vietnamese factories were mere boondoggles, much of the Soviet aid was wasted.

Le Duan and his colleagues thought they were "building socialism." As the Soviet Union and the nations of Eastern Europe discovered, the concrete of socialism crumbles. There is too much sand in it from inefficiencies inherent in the system and from the way the system contradicts human nature. The sheer profligacy of the Vietnamese version hastened its demise. The regime ended up simply printing money to pay the subsidies.

By 1986, when Le Duan died, the Vietnamese economy was on the verge of collapse and there was a crisis of public confidence in the Party's ability to govern. Inflation was out of control at 600 to 700 percent a year. The currency was becoming more worthless by the month, the official exchange rate 1,500 dong to the dollar, the black market rate 5,000. The stores were bare of consumer items. Vietnamese waited in long lines at the state rice shops for their monthly rations because the storage and transportation systems were breaking down too; rice was often simply not available. A Russian chemical engineer working for the United Nations flew from Hanoi to Ho Chi Minh City (as the capital of the South and its environs were renamed after the American war) with a delegation of high-ranking Vietnamese officials that year. He was astonished to see these senior officials, all Party members, hauling bags of rice back on the return trip because rice was five times more expensive on the free market in Hanoi. Although people were not starving as in Africa, hunger and malnutrition had become chronic in the Red River delta and in Central Vietnam.

The reformers prevailed just in time at the Sixth Party Congress in December 1986. (The Vietnamese Communist Party meets in general conclave about every five years.) Nguyen Van Linh, a Northerner who had spent the entire French and American wars fighting in the South and who in 1982 had also been pushed out of the Politburo by Le Duan for opposing the headlong rush to socialism, was elected general secretary. *Doi moi* and the sobering-up from the victory binge began.

The Vietnamese boast that they were the first among the former array of socialist countries to launch drastic economic reforms to convert their system to a predominantly free market economy. In 1987 and 1988, while Mikhail Gorbachev was still trying to redeem the unredeemable centralized economy of the Soviet Union with *perestroika*, before the earthquake of change and the "shock therapy" free market measures adopted in Poland and elsewhere in Eastern Europe, the Vietnamese were on their way.

Rationing and subsidized prices for rice and all other commodities were abolished. People were told they would have to buy what they needed in the open market. Capitalism was legalized and private enterprise encouraged. The currency was freed to find its true value; the artificial exchange rate was ended, and the dong was permitted to float at approximately the black market rate. In order to counter inflation by shrinking the money supply, the government stopped printing money. The borders were opened to trade, and a liberal foreign investment law was passed to try to attract capital from Western and Asian capitalist nations. Agriculture was decollectivized. The farmers were given back the land under fifteen-year contracts, granted in exchange for amounts of rice fixed at the outset, the equivalent of a land tax in a Western country. The rest of the harvest belonged to the farmer to sell to whomever he wished.

Stalin's economic model for industry went the way of collectivization. About forty big industrial projects—a new iron and steel center, a tractor factory, a heavy machinery plant—were abandoned. Emphasis was shifted to light industry and to the support of agriculture and the production of consumer goods. Centralized planning was drastically curtailed. Factory managers were told that they were on their own—that they would have to decide what to make, find their customers, pay free market prices for whatever raw materials they needed, and make a profit or go bankrupt.

By the summer of 1989, prices had stabilized, stores were filled with a spectrum of goods, inflation had fallen from 1988's 600 to 700 percent to a projected 25 percent for the year (it was held to 35 percent for all of 1989), rice production was up considerably, and the country was able to export rice in quantity for the first time since the 1930s.

Nguyen Cong Quang, the director of the Foreign Press Center, an old-fashioned Vietnamese official who believed in abstemious living for a public servant and rode a secondhand bicycle around Hanoi, asked what I wanted to see. Now that I finally had a chance to see the North, war had been replaced as the national preoccupation by economics and the changes being forced on the society by the conversion to a free market economy. I decided to hew to the journalist's old rule of following the main story to see where it led and what it would tell about the country. Initially it led to quite a few factories and construction sites.

One Saturday afternoon went into a visit to a carpet factory in a Hanoi suburb that was exporting rugs to West Germany to earn hard currency, another Saturday afternoon into a tour of a fan factory with a ready market at home. The pride of Vietnam, the Vietnam People's Army (called the North Vietnamese Army or NVA during the war by the American military), was being rapidly demobilized by half, from a million down to 500,000, its generals scrambling to find ways to support themselves and the officers and men of their institution.

The 14,000-man corps that once had overseen the building of roads and bridges for one of the engineering marvels of modern military history—the Ho Chi Minh Trail, the great rain-forest highway grid that had sustained the war in the South with men and matériel—had become an "economic army," in the words of its commanding general. The corps was dispersed all over Vietnam,

laying railroads northeast of Hanoi to transport coal, mining apatite, a source of phosphates for fertilizer, and quarrying marble for export along the Central Coast, growing coffee on mountain plantations in the Central Highlands of the South. A hot dawn-to-dusk trip west along Route 6 from Hanoi to Hoa Binh, the site of a famous French defeat that was a harbinger of Dien Bien Phu, was invested in a visit to an engineer division of the corps that was the lead task force in the largest hydroelectric project in the country, set in a gorge of the Black River above the town. The burnt sienna water of the misnamed river metamorphosed into a plume of gray as it crashed into the side of the main spillway of the dam and shot up into the sun.

During the war, Haiphong, the chief port for the North, sixty miles east of Hanoi, had the distinction of being, along with Hanoi and Saigon, one of three Vietnamese cities on the American mental map. The hold of a ship could probably be filled with the collected texts of the speeches and congressional hearings, the columns and editorials arguing whether to bomb Haiphong more or to bomb it less, whether to close its approaches with mines, as Lyndon Johnson refused to do and as Richard Nixon finally did in 1972. Memories create expectations, and I came to Haiphong with visions of a defiant Vietnamese Marseilles. To my surprise, Haiphong was not a city on the sea. It turned out that the port was eleven miles inland from the South China Sea up a silt-laden channel. The impressively large oceangoing ships I had anticipated did not exist; there were only ordinary freighters moored at dockyards that were hardly bustling. The mines were gone. The U.S. Navy had sent minesweeping ships to clear the harbor channel under the Paris Agreement of 1973. The Vietnamese Navy had finished the task by finding the mines the Americans had missed. The bomb damage had been repaired. Yet, given the history of the city, it seemed ironic when I encountered in Haiphong my first "Red capitalist."

This freshly minted Vietnamese appellation connotes a state factory manager who is displaying initiative and making money by running a factory like a shrewd private firm. Mrs. Phi Yen, the

director of the Haiphong Export Sea Products Processing Enterprise, also known as Factory No. 42, typified this conventional
route to success under *doi moi.* In 1986 she had persuaded a
Japanese firm to let her have $1,250,000 worth of processing and
freezing equipment and to pay off the debt in frozen shrimp.
Technically, the factory was owned by the city of Haiphong and
Mrs. Yen was a city employee. Actually, she was in charge and split
the profits with the city authorities. The shrimp in the packets she
pulled from the freezers were uniformly large and professionally
packaged. So were the fillets of fish—red and pink snapper, red
emperor, and grouper, among the fifteen varieties.

An inquiry about newly sanctioned private enterprise led to a
spectacle of guerrilla capitalism in the countryside just south of
Hanoi. A forty-three-year-old former government construction-
specialist-turned-entrepreneur had leased a pond from the local
authorities, filled it in with sand and dirt, and was erecting on the
site a factory to stamp out plastic roofing sheets. The construction
workers, barefoot men in tattered shorts who had no cranes, were
moving his heavy stamping machinery into place entirely by hand.
They would tie a hunk of machinery with ropes to a thick,
rough-hewn pole and then, with half a dozen men at each end of
the pole, count loudly in unison to heave-ho and lift simultaneously. The temperature in the afternoon sun exceeded 100
degrees.

Most of the foreign businessmen I met in Hanoi while exploring
this Vietnam in transition—the last reservoir of cheap labor in
Southeast Asia at 64 million people and an educated potential
work force too because of a decent primary school system—were
from the so-called "lesser dragons" of Asian economic power—
Hong Kong, Taiwan, Singapore, South Korea. They were being
properly cautious about putting down their money. Not so a
young Vietnamese-American named Nguyen Tri. He had made his
bet, despite the U.S. economic embargo on Vietnam. The son of
a prosperous family on the Saigon government side, Tri had left
Vietnam a year before the collapse in 1975, graduated from the
University of Oklahoma, and worked for nearly ten years for Shell

Oil in Houston. His mother-in-law had moved to Bangkok and gone into business in Vietnam after 1986. She had persuaded Tri to abandon his career in Houston and become the more or less resident manager of her multitudinous affairs. The exploits of Nguyen Tri's mother-in-law, a tenacious Vietnamese woman, made would-be foreign venture capitalists seem tame indeed.

Tri's principal concern when I first met him was a ruby mine that his mother-in-law and a Thai general had bought in partnership with influential and unnamed Vietnamese. The mine was in the mountains up toward the Chinese border, 105 miles and eight hours of rough road northwest of Hanoi. Tri had shipped in an imposing Japanese four-wheel-drive vehicle to get to the place. There was no electricity, no potable water, and no housing beyond huts at the mine, he said. Vietnamese and Chinese claim jumpers who did not mind the lack of amenities were also digging up rubies. In an attempt to stop the theft, Tri had signed a contract with the Vietnamese Army division commander for the area to guard the premises. He faced the daunting task of hauling up generators and other equipment, building housing, and assembling a staff and work force to extract the rubies.

One afternoon the flight from Bangkok brought in the first of the staff—half a dozen Thais who were specialists in gem mining. Tri told me with amusement that the Thais objected to the Government Guest House, where he was temporarily housing them in Hanoi, and wanted to move to a regular hotel where they could bring in prostitutes. But he was determined to keep them out of trouble and get them to the mine. A couple of days later the Japanese four-wheeler took them all away to the huts and the rubies in the Vietnamese Wild West.

The other face of *doi moi* was at a town called Hai Duong on the road to Haiphong. The roads of the North are another of its anachronisms. The main route east from Hanoi to Haiphong is the same two-lane strip it was in the French era. In the meantime the population has soared beyond the imagination of the colonial road engineers. The Red River delta has become one of the most crowded rural environments in Asia. Tens of millions of people live in this delta shaped like an inverted funnel that is only about eighty miles wide at its mouth along the coast and just one hundred miles long as it progressively narrows its way back to the spout where the Red River and its tributaries emerge from the mountains northwest of Hanoi. The Vietnamese have also partially joined the modern world by acquiring a lot of wheels. Although there is a railroad from Hanoi to the port of Haiphong, trucks and vans haul most of the goods and produce between the two cities. The big vehicles sometimes roar pell-mell for a stretch, sometimes crawl because they have to skirt a stream of bicycles and motorcycles moving three and four abreast on their right near the side of the road.

This stream of lesser "wheels" is not the only obstacle. Flat, hard surfaces are at a premium in the countryside of the Red River delta, where everyone competes for space. Many farmers are too poor to have a backyard or a terrace on which to dry their rice straw and perform other agricultural chores. They therefore spread out the straw—and sometimes unhusked rice too, or whatever they want to sort or dry—on the tarmac. Custom dictates that the drivers avoid mashing the produce and whoever may be raking it.

The pump factory at Hai Duong had been a model until recently, but it had been a model with a Newark-like, down-at-the-heels look of broken windowpanes and hunks of steel discarded here and there. In its original incarnation before World War II the site had been a French distillery, part of the alcohol monopoly established by the colonial authorities to help defray the cost of civilizing the natives. The population of each community, such as Hai Duong, had to purchase a preset quantity of alcohol whether they drank it or not. One of the buildings still bore the lettering Société Française des Distilleries de l'Indochine. The factory headquarters was in an old villa that had been the home of the French distillery manager. Nguyen Ngoc Can, the factory director, a Southerner who had emigrated to the North after the end of the

French war in 1954, and his assistants received us around an oilcloth-covered table in the former dining room that was now their conference room.

Overnight, the world had turned upside down. The Ministry of Engineering and Metals in Hanoi, which had always been the great paternal figure, became useless, capable only of suggesting guidelines that might or might not make sense. What kind of pumps to manufacture, who was likely to buy them, and what price to charge became questions Mr. Can and his associates were supposed to answer. The cost of steel with which to make pumps tripled because it had to be bought at the open market price rather than at the formerly subsidized one. Yet Mr. Can could not immediately start demanding three times more for pumps, because potential customers didn't have that kind of money in the current economic environment. Initially he got stuck with 110 high-capacity electric pumps, capable of moving 1,000 to 4,000 cubic meters of water per hour, as leftovers from 1988 production. (A cubic meter is equivalent to nearly 4 cubic feet.) He then made a misjudgment that compounded his problems. In 1989 the factory turned out an additional 300 electric pumps in the 1,000-cubic-meters-per-hour category on the assumption that there would be a market for them. A mere fifty had been sold.

Why couldn't the factory sell its pumps? The return of the land to the farmers under fifteen-year contracts had undermined its raison d'être, Mr. Can explained. Prior policy had assumed that all irrigation was a government responsibility to be managed centrally at the cooperative or district level, hence the requirement for big pumps. Under *doi moi*, while the authorities remained responsible for major dikes and other large-scale irrigation tasks, village irrigation had been turned over to the farmers. Individual peasants or even groups of families banding together hardly needed to shift 1,000 cubic meters of water in an hour, nor could they afford to run pumps of this size.

Mr. Can and his associates were experimenting with a new 50-cubic-meters-per-hour pump aimed at the farmer market. It could be run with a portable four-horsepower generator produced by another factory with which the Hai Duong plant was cooperating. They had also been resorting to stopgap measures to survive. Teams of workers had been sent out to service pumps already sold, textile machinery was being repaired and assembled, and the factory had reduced its prices for pumps four times to attempt to stimulate sales, despite the fact that higher-priced steel and lower-priced pumps did not add up to profits.

Economic realities had begun to assert themselves. The lack of orders had forced the plant to reduce operations to 60 percent of capacity. The normal workweek in Vietnam is six days. That June Mr. Can had put his 856 workers on a four-day one. He had chosen a reduced workweek over layoffs to try to give his employees a subsistence wage because layoffs and bankruptcies of state factories brought on by the new economic policies had become a dread of Vietnamese workers. Although all statistics in Vietnam were suspect—one wondered how the government could possibly compile accurate ones in a country of such poor communications that dwells in the precomputer, prephotocopy age of pencils and dog-eared carbon paper—unemployment was said to be running at about 25 percent, roughly 7 million out of an urban and rural work force estimated at 30 million people. The problem was just as bad in the countryside, where it was hidden in the villages as underemployment, as it was in the towns and cities.

Neither Mr. Can nor any of the other men at the table in the former dining room of the French distillery manager appeared to have gained much financially in the course of their careers fighting wars and making pumps. Mr. Can had first joined the Viet Minh underground while a teenager during World War II. Now he was wearing an inexpensive Japanese watch. The Party secretary for the factory, a mechanical engineer, laughed in derision when I asked if a joint venture with foreign investors might be a way out of their troubles. His laugh suggested that no foreign investor would want a Newark in Hai Duong.

On a wall behind the table, hung around a portrait of Stalin shaking hands with Lenin, were red banners with gold lettering, the Vietnamese national colors, which the factory had won for excel-

ling at Stalin's economic model. Among these mementos of the
glory years was a 1985 award from the Council of Ministers, the
equivalent of a cabinet in the Vietnamese system of government,
for victory in a five-year competition for production consistency
and quality.

What was worse, I asked Mr. Can, fighting the French in
Interzone Five, the central coastal command where he had spent
the first Vietnamese war for independence, or directing a state
factory during *doi moi*?

"It was easier in Interzone Five," he said.

As the Red River delta has become one of the most densely
populated rural environments in Asia, so Hanoi has become one
of the most crowded urban ones. In the central sector of the city
the population density runs to about 520 persons per acre, one of
the highest on earth. Some of the worst crowding occurs in the
ancient part of Hanoi, where thirty-six picturesque streets, so
narrow they are actually lanes, are knit together into a section just
above the city's most famous lake, the Lake of the Restored Sword.
Many of the low-lying one- and two-story buildings there are
hundreds of years old. With plumbing in them virtually nonexis-
tent, a nightly ritual is to take the children down to the sidewalk
before bedtime to urinate. The number of Vietnamese packed into
once-spacious villas in the former European sections is just as
astonishing. The Australian Embassy, in need of more room for its
staff, leased two adjacent buildings from the Hanoi city government. When the Vietnamese residents were evicted so that the
buildings could be refurbished, the Australians discovered to their
horror that 127 Vietnamese had been living in just one of the
two-story houses.

In principle—that is, according to government regulation—
everyone in the city is entitled to six square meters (21.5 square
feet) of living space. Married couples are officially entitled to a bit
more than double that, with additional space supposedly allotted
as children come along. In fact, when young people marry they
normally move in with the wife's or the husband's family, which-

ever is most willing to take them, and then pack in the children as they appear. Parents have resigned themselves to the situation, progressively giving up more space as each child marries and the grandchildren are born. There is a quid pro quo. The Confucian ethic and Vietnamese tradition say that children should look after parents when they grow old, and the only real social security that anyone has in present-day Vietnam is the family. The advantage that both the Confucian ethic and the housing shortage provides for young marrieds is live-in babysitters and nursemaids for the next generation: A sight almost as common as a grandmother bathing a child in a tin tub at curbside (the crowding means that much of life has to be lived outdoors) is that of a grandfather sitting in a canvas chair on a sidewalk on a stifling evening, cooling a baby in his lap with a hand-held fan. Where bathrooms and kitchens are available, they are normally communal affairs, with the four to five families involved drawing up schedules as to who will clean in a given week.

Not surprisingly, the most common civil dispute in Hanoi concerns housing. "There is a housing war in Vietnam," a prominent newspaper editor said when I interviewed him. The ruckus typically starts when one family tries to build its own kitchen or walls off a portion of a house or an apartment, inconveniencing others. Because of corruption in local government, if the dispute is then taken to the district People's Committee, it usually gets settled in favor of the side that pays the most money. (Government administrative bodies in Vietnam, both urban and rural, are known as People's Committees. The Hanoi city government, for example, is called the Hanoi People's Committee.) An appeal to higher authority normally does not alter the outcome. The Hanoi People's Committee will tell the district committee to "look into this matter," and the district committee will reply that it already has. Persistence may result in the city government's sending an investigator, but again his efforts frequently do not bring justice. Some housing disputes become so heated that the losing parties appeal all the way to the National Assembly.

No. 104 Tran Hung Dao Street was the most controversial

address in Hanoi while I was there. A cabal of senior civil servants had gotten eleven families evicted from older housing on the site and arranged to have it demolished, and had a new apartment building put up, with government funds, under the guise of a housing experiment. The nature of the experiment was that they moved into the attractive four-story building. As I drove by on a summer afternoon, I could see the residents on their terraces overlooking the wide thoroughfare. *Labor,* one of the more outspoken newspapers in Hanoi, discovered the scam and published an article exposing it. The outcry led to an order from the Council of Ministers for an investigation. The civil servant tenants, all high-ranking people at the vice-ministerial and deputy head of department level, were embarrassed at having their names in the newspaper, but not embarrassed enough to surrender their swindled apartments. They brought their influence to bear. The investigation was sufficiently inconclusive for them to avoid eviction notices.

The government's proposed remedy for the housing crush—the erection of new apartment blocks in the suburbs—has so far proven elusive. The authorities lack funds to build enough housing to approach demand, which keeps rising as the population does, and the new buildings deteriorate rapidly. Just how rapidly is readily apparent from a local custom of dating a building by putting the year it was finished above the entrance or under the rooftop. Buildings dated 1985 look as if someone misdated them by a decade or two. Shoddy construction plays to a climate—with temperature fluctuations from the high 90s in summer to the low 40s in winter, constant humidity, and frequent rains—that would be hard on any materials. The apartment blocks are put up with concrete slabs, a standard Soviet building technique that is in principle quite sturdy, but the concrete is commonly too soft to withstand the elements. Cement is the hardening agent in concrete, and the workers and officials in charge of the construction organizations steal as much cement as they can to sell on the free market. A new bridge erected at the port of Haiphong collapsed because

30 to 40 percent of the cement that was supposed to go into the concrete had been pilfered.

Finland, one of the two non-Communist European countries that did not cut off aid to Vietnam after the invasion of Cambodia (Sweden was the other), is trying to ameliorate the lives of Hanoians by helping the city build a new water supply system to replace the decrepit French-built one. When I was there, stacks of big cast-iron, concrete-lined water pipes awaiting installation were a sign to passersby that Finland cared. Pressure in the old French system is so low from cracked pipes and loose joints that hundreds of thousands of people have to collect their water in buckets from shallow sidewalk wells created by punching holes in the underground pipes and running taps off them. Some of the wells are individual sidewalk bomb shelters left over from the American war.

The wells and the general water supply system are both severely contaminated whenever there is flooding from heavy rains or a typhoon. Polluted surface water surges first into the wells and then into the water supply system through the holes cut in the pipes for the taps. The primitive sewer system left behind by the French worsens the pollution. The colonizers built a sewer system only for their part of the city, ignoring the sections where the Vietnamese lived. Modern cities also separate sanitary sewers from storm drains to carry off rainwater. The French colonial system ran both into the same set of pipes, and the pipes empty into the city's lakes and the Red River. When the drains are overwhelmed by flooding, the sewage has nowhere to go but back into the city.

Hai Ba Trung is a postwar hospital, built to serve the population of southeast Hanoi. It took ten years to complete because of the shortage of funds and materials, and finally opened in 1984. The hospital and its director, Prof. Dr. Nguyen Van Xang, epitomize the hope and the sadness of health care in Vietnam. The country does not want for doctors in the cities and larger towns, where living conditions are most attractive for professionals. Vietnam graduates about two thousand doctors a year from its seven medical schools, the leading ones being in Hanoi and Ho Chi Minh City. Not all are as capable as Professor Xang, but by and large medical education in Vietnam, which harkens back to the original medical faculty founded by the French at the University of Hanoi, is considered good. The rub is the daunting conditions doctors face in practicing the healing art because of the lack of medications and adequate equipment. Professor Xang did not permit himself, or the 150 physicians who worked under him at Hai Ba Trung, to get discouraged. "You have to scrounge for that," he said in French when he mentioned one of the scarce antibiotics he needed to treat tuberculosis.

The hospital has six hundred beds and under Professor Xang's direction concentrates on infectious diseases, internal medicine, and plastic surgery to repair birth defects and burns from accidents. Professor Xang had made it a teaching hospital as well because he was also deputy chief of the Department of Surgery at the Hanoi Medical School. "We lost a lot of time on the war—we're a little old," he said. "We're trying to help the sick and to train young M.D.s. In our country it's the young who count."

If fleetness is a virtue of youth, it was one that Professor Xang had not lost with fifty-nine years. A figure of fine-drawn slimness in white coat and cap, with gray hair that he let grow long over his ears and down his neck, he was light on his feet, plastic sandals flying, as he guided visitors around his hospital. One of the first stops on the tour was at three secondhand kidney dialysis machines, which Professor Xang had brought back from Holland at the beginning of 1989 after six months of studying kidney disease at a Catholic university there. The Dutch hospital connected to the university had been in the process of replacing its machines and had let him have these.

"They're good machines," he said, and he wanted to use them to create a kidney dialysis center for the North. "I can easily manage the technique—my young colleagues too." He currently had a patient in the hospital with kidney failure brought on by falciparum malaria. The problem was acquiring disposable supplies to make the machines function. The Dutch professor he had worked with had given him twenty filters. He had used up eight and was hoarding the remaining twelve for the most urgent cases. He also needed solution. To import a single filter cost the equivalent of ten dollars in foreign currency he could not get.

So it went through the rest of the hospital: the work always a hodgepodge of use your imagination, make do with what you have, and be grateful for what you've been given. Professor Xang unfailingly named each donor and his or her country of origin. "Coulter Counter, from Jessie Sharp, a woman doctor from London who came to see me in 1984. Freezer, aid from a West German organization called Bread for the World." One of the sterilizers he had—another gift—was of reasonably modern German vintage; a second was an old metal box from the French days, modified for electricity. The thermostats on top were broken. "You need experience to use it," Professor Xang said. A small microscope to examine urine specimens literally dated from the nineteenth century. "You would have left it in a museum, but we can see a little better than with our eyes," he noted with a smile.

A triumph of the imagination was on display in the second-floor laboratory of the hospital's microbiologist, Dr. Le Van Phung. Dr. Phung was a cheerful man of thirty-six, a former student and protégé of Professor Xang. He had recently returned from a three-month internship in Japan. His work was critical to the hospital. He grew cultures with specimens from patients with infectious diseases and tested antibiotics against them, enabling Professor Xang and the other physicians to use what medications they could get with maximum effect. Dr. Phung had needed a crucial tool—a centrifuge. He proudly displayed the Le Van Phung model. The little electric motor and drive shaft had been obtained by stripping the blades off a small Vietnamese fan. The fluorescent lights over Dr. Phung's laboratory table were too weak for him to adequately study his cultures. On clear days he carried culture and microscope over to a window.

Professor Xang's plastic sandals skittered up and down stairs as the tour continued. Two rooms were air-conditioned, but to preserve equipment, not for the comfort of patients. One room held an ultrasound device employed in the treatment of tumors and liver ailments, the other a Japanese machine for taking electroencephalograms, which monitor the electrical activity of the brain. The air conditioners were mounted in the walls behind cagelike bars to discourage thieves. A refrigerator in the blood bank was also kept locked because it contained eggs, bread, and milk for small meals given as rewards to donors. Recruiting donors was difficult in Vietnam because of a popular misconception that the body does not regenerate the blood given and one will fall ill as a result. Professor Xang said he also wished that he had the means of testing blood for AIDS, although so far there was thought to be little of it in the country. The greatest danger from a blood transfusion was hepatitis B, which infects perhaps 15 percent of the population.

Throughout the tour Professor Xang paid no attention to the hospital's sanitary conditions because he was accustomed to them. Susan and I were assailed by what happens when a hospital has little money for maintenance and no antiseptic cleansing materials: grime-covered floors and walls, toilets that reeked, showers that had long ago ceased functioning. Crocks of water stood next to the showers with pails for the patients to use in dousing themselves.

The last stop was the intensive care ward, a single large room where making do ended. Even though a charwoman was moving a mop around on the concrete floor, the place was as unsanitary and foul smelling as the rest of the hospital. The six patients in the intensive care ward, two children and four adults, some of whom had infectious diseases like typhoid fever, lay close together on beds with straw mats. There were no sheets or mattresses. Family members stood around to do the nursing chores and comfort them. One of the patients was a young man, the case Professor Xang had mentioned earlier, who had failing kidneys from falciparum malaria. Professor Xang was going to perform dialysis on the patient that evening and had prepared his own solution, displaying a plastic bagful. Because the solution lacked an ingredient that it was supposed to have, he was not certain it would work.

The smallest patient in the room was a fourteen-month-old girl, feverish and asleep. Her parents sat on a bench beside her cot. Professor Xang explained that the child had an infection of the bloodstream and he needed a cephalosporin-type antibiotic to save her. (One is commonly sold in the United States under the brand name Keflex.) Susan and I offered to pay for it. "You can't buy it in Hanoi," he said. We tried. To our regret—and the regret haunts still—he was right.

In the car afterward Duong Quang Thang, the other guide-interpreter assigned to us by the Foreign Press Center, said that when his wife had given birth to their son, there had been two women to a bed and three infants to a cot. Thang had had to take two weeks off from work—a normal practice for Vietnamese husbands when their wives give birth—to bring food three times a day, changes of clothing, and water for drinking and washing. The hospitals do have kitchens, he said, but no one would want to eat the food they provide. What was most striking about his story was that position and salary do not provide an escape, for Thang, thirty years old, was a middle-level civil servant with a good income, and his wife was also a professional.

With the hope that free enterprise might improve health care, the reformers got two laws through the National Assembly while I was in Hanoi. One authorized hospitals to charge patients who could afford to pay for services and medications. Another gave doctors the right to set up private practices after normal working hours and to operate private clinics. Although the laws were clearly going to bring about far more privatizing of medicine, to some extent they legalized the existing conditions. Professor Xang had explained to us that he asked families with means to buy medications so that he could save the limited amount he had for the neediest.

There is no quick solution to the fundamental health problems of the country. The turmoil in the wake of the American war and the American-Chinese boycott had delayed a campaign sponsored by UNICEF and the UN's World Health Organization (WHO) to vaccinate all children against the six main diseases of tuberculosis, whooping cough, diphtheria, tetanus, tetanus toxoid, and polio.

The campaign was now making good progress, but the Vietnamese do not expect to eradicate polio until the year 2005. A second campaign, this one also sponsored by WHO, was being waged against another major killer of children—diarrhea. Mothers in the villages were being taught to stop the dehydration that brings death by the simple method of administering oral rehydration salts—a sachet of glucose, sodium bicarbonate, salt, and potassium chloride dissolved in boiled water. The strategy behind both campaigns, to use limited resources in a way that would benefit the greatest number, was intelligent but could offer no protection against diseases that were more costly to eradicate.

Before leaving Washington, Susan and I had been warned by a tropical medicine specialist, Dr. Martin Wolfe, to get a shot for Japanese encephalitis when we reached Bangkok and to carry enough vaccine along to Hanoi for a second shot two weeks later to complete the immunization. (Because the Japanese manufacturer feared lawsuits by litigation-prone Americans, the vaccine was available in the United States only to military personnel and to civilian officials working with the military.) "You'll see cases of Japanese encephalitis when you get to Hanoi," Dr. Wolfe said. We asked how we would recognize them. "They will probably be children," he said. "They'll be asleep and they won't wake up."

Epidemics of this mosquito-borne disease, which inflames the brain, strike Hanoi and the Red River delta during the hot months. The victims are usually children because children have not yet built up much resistance, which adults have as an ironic benefit of infections of dengue and lesser fevers. There is no cure for Japanese encephalitis, and those who survive are often incapacitated. Dr. Wolfe was right. We saw two victims in one hospital, a baby boy in a deep coma and a boy of twelve in the terrible sleep, his father, a doctor, standing distraught beside the bed.

To protect its children against Japanese encephalitis would cost Vietnam two dollars in imported vaccine for each immunization and use up the entire national health budget. Vaccine for the curse of hepatitis B is also beyond the country's means. Dr. Judith Ladinsky, who teaches preventive medicine at the University of

Wisconsin in Madison and heads a humanitarian organization called the U.S. Committee for Scientific Cooperation with Vietnam, is trying to help the Vietnamese get around the expense of importation by showing them how to develop and manufacture their own vaccines. With her assistance, the Vietnamese have so far developed a hepatitis B vaccine at the laboratory level. The road from laboratory to working vaccination programs will, however, take years. There is no vaccine against the blindness that results from a deficiency of vitamin A. It comes from the malnutrition of poverty. The blindness is irreversible if it is not caught in time, and it was frequent among the ragged children, many with skin sores, whom I saw whenever I went to one of the villages in the Red River delta.

As part of a 1987 agreement with the United States to search for the remains of American war dead, the Vietnamese had been told they would get humanitarian help from private American organizations, so-called Non-Governmental Organizations, or "NGOs" in the parlance of international aid. (I found no evidence while I was in Vietnam to support the missing-in-action theory one often encounters in the United States that Vietnam continues to hold American prisoners. The Vietnamese suffered hundreds of thousands of missing in action of their own during the American war, so many that there is no precise figure. An estimated 3 million Vietnamese from both sides, combatants and noncombatants alike, are believed to have perished.) The humanitarian assistance that has come as a result of the agreement—some prosthetic devices, some antibiotics, occasional trips by surgical teams—is a token, given the country's enormous needs. Only large-scale governmental aid from the Western countries and Japan, which the U.S. and China kept out by diplomatic pressure, could make a difference.

The one European country besides Finland that was ignoring the embargo, Sweden, provided the sole source of significant medical aid to Vietnam, about $8 million a year. The 400-bed Vietnam-Sweden Children's Hospital, built in a Hanoi suburb between 1975 and 1980, was the single adequately equipped and supplied hospital I saw in the whole country. It had five modern operating rooms, incubators, and an ample quantity of medications. Although the Vietnamese were in charge, the Swedes had wisely followed up the building and equipping of the hospital by helping to run it. A Swedish doctor, a nursing supervisor, and technicians worked with Prof. Dr. Nguyen Thi Nhan, a woman Vietnamese pediatrician, and her staff. The hospital was also the only one I visited in Vietnam that was clean.

The day after we saw Hai Ba Trung, I asked Thang to take us to Bach Mai, which Richard Nixon had once made the best-known hospital in Vietnam when it was hit by a B-52 during his Christmas 1972 bombing of Hanoi. The bombing is old news now, and as old news Bach Mai no longer attracts prominent visitors. Prof. Dr. Tran Do Trinh, the deputy director, a pleasant-spoken man of fifty-eight, had been lying awake in the basement when the bombs struck at two A.M. on December 22, 1972. He had delivered a lecture on rheumatic heart disease earlier that night but could not fall asleep because he was so tense from the reverberation of the bombing and the racket of the Vietnamese antiaircraft batteries. The smaller U.S. fighter-bombers had first come over the city in a preliminary raid at the beginning of his lecture at nine P.M. Then the big bombers arrived after midnight. The explosive force of the seven bombs that fell simultaneously on the cardiology department collapsed the floors above into the basement. Eleven of the people around Professor Trinh were killed, most of them doctors, medical students, and nurses who were on duty to care for the patients being sheltered in the basement. The dermatology department across the courtyard was hit harder. Seventeen died there.

A number of well-known people visited the hospital right after the bombing to commiserate. Even Henry Kissinger, then Nixon's special assistant for national security affairs, came to see the wreckage when he flew to Hanoi after the signing of the Paris Agreement of January 1973. The late Le Duc Tho, chief Vietnamese delegate at the Paris negotiations, escorted him. Professor Trinh recalled that Kissinger expressed his regret and said the B-52 had been trying to hit a small French airfield a little more than half a mile away that was being used by the Vietnamese as a helicopter base.

It took two weeks to dig out the dead. An American humanitarian group called Medical Aid for Indochina gave the cardiology department $200,000 worth of equipment—a defibrillator, a pacemaker, an electrocardiograph, and Vietnam's first echocardiograph, a simple one-dimensional type. The rebuilding took eleven years. The hospital celebrated the completion with fireworks on the eleventh anniversary night, December 22, 1983.

Bach Mai, with one thousand beds, was the main hospital for the North. It was also the principal teaching hospital for Hanoi Medical School, with three hundred and fifty doctors assigned to it and eight hundred medical students who came each day for classes. Professor Trinh was the second member of his family to serve as its deputy director. His grandfather, a general practitioner, had been the assistant to the French director back in the 1930s. Bach Mai was called the René Robin then, after a governor general of Indochina, and Professor Trinh's grandfather actually ran the hospital while the French doctor taught at the colonial medical faculty. Professor Trinh's own road to becoming one of Vietnam's eminent cardiologists led through Dien Bien Phu, where, while still a medical student, he performed as a battlefield surgeon.

Despite its position as a national hospital, Bach Mai bore out everything we had seen at Hai Ba Trung and all that Thang had said about Vietnamese hospitals in general. The cardiology ward had fifty-five beds, but a normal patient load of eighty; three women lay in one bed in the women's section. Saddest for Professor Trinh, the opportunities to improve the hospital had ended when the publicity about the bombing was over. He had not been able to replace any of the equipment he received from Medical Aid for Indochina in the 1970s. (The organization no longer exists.) Vietnam's first echocardiograph was now an old machine that no longer functioned properly; he thought wistfully of a new bidimensional echocardiograph with Doppler in color. His assistant, Dr. Nguyen Tuyet Minh, a woman cardiologist who had studied in the Netherlands, pointed to a young man on a bed who was one of her patients. He was a fine scientist who had a congenital heart disease, she said. She could save him if she had modern equipment and medications, but she didn't have either and he was going to die.

Henry Kissinger might have regretted the bombing of Bach Mai Hospital during the Christmas 1972 raids, but he and his president had known there was a good chance that incidents like this would occur. Richard Nixon sent the B-52s to Hanoi to try to get his way. He thought he could frighten the Vietnamese Communists so that they would never again launch a major offensive in the South and would leave in place the pro-American government of Nguyen Van Thieu that the Nixon administration was attempting to preserve in Saigon. The president and Kissinger had been told by the military leadership that if they used the big bombers against military targets in and around the city, "collateral damage" to civilian areas was virtually inevitable. For this reason, Nixon's predecessor, Lyndon Johnson, had always refused to employ the B-52s over Hanoi. Targeting an airfield half a mile from a hospital meant that if the crew of the B-52, under enormous stress from the antiaircraft artillery and the Soviet-made surface-to-air missiles the Vietnamese were shooting at them, made a minute error in bomb drop, they might well hit the hospital—and so they did.

Four nights later, the night after Christmas 1972, the crew of another B-52 committed the same predictable error and obliterated three adjoining houses on Kham Thien Street, just south of the Hanoi railroad station. Because of poor record keeping no one knew precisely how many people had died there, but the number was believed to exceed those killed at Bach Mai. In honor of the dead, the houses had not been rebuilt. There was an iron grille fence in front of the missing homes with their numbers on a gate: 47–49–51. Behind the gate was a statue of a young woman carrying a child in her arms—a memorial to a Vietnamese mother who perished with her family in one of the houses.

The Vietnamese admitted they had been frightened when the B-52s came. The eight-engine jet Stratofortresses that laid carpets of bombs seemed like science-fiction death machines. They were said to fly so high that the surface-to-air missiles, called SAMs, could not reach them, and they carried special electronic gear to confuse the radar that guided the SAMs and the conventional antiaircraft artillery. Until the arrival of the B-52s, the bombing of targets in downtown Hanoi had also been relatively light, and so the sudden turn for the worse was in itself unnerving. Despite their fear, the Vietnamese reacted with the David-versus-Goliath reflex that is natural to them. They hurled missiles and fired antiaircraft artillery and discovered they could bring down some of these awesome planes. (Thang, at the time a boy of thirteen who had been evacuated to the suburbs like many of the children in the city, saw one B-52 that was shot down crash in flames into a rice field near the village where he was staying.) When the battle with the B-52s was over, the Vietnamese regarded it in a perspective that Nixon had not anticipated.

The exhibits at the Army Museum in Hanoi told the tale from the Vietnamese side. The early exhibits recalled the beginnings of the country's modern war for independence in the struggle against the French. There was a photograph of Vo Nguyen Giap address-ing the first guerrilla band of the future Vietnam People's Army in 1944 in the mountains near the China border. The lycée teacher who would wear four stars was dressed in a trilby hat, a business suit, and sandals. In a case nearby was his first pistol, one of the big semiautomatic Mausers from the factory at Oberndorf am Neckar favored by Chinese armies in the 1920s and '30s.

As a visitor worked his way forward through the exhibits of the American war, he gradually found himself in the midst of the battle of the B-52s. The initial encounter was a pile of wreckage in the museum yard, the remains of one of the bombers shot down on December 18, 1972, the first night of the raids. Nearby was a torn section of fuselage from another B-52 with the emblem of the Strategic Air Command, a bolt of lightning grasped in a fist, painted on it. Inside the main room of the museum the battle unfolded. There was a large photograph of Nixon discussing strategy with Kissinger, pictures of B-52s in flight, streams of bombs falling from the bomb bays, the rubble at Bach Mai and Kham Thien Street, and then one photograph after another of

Vietnamese in flak jackets and helmets firing antiaircraft guns, tracking bombers on radar, launching missiles. They had to defeat the planes.

The Vietnamese did not really defeat the B-52s. Although their antiaircraft defenses inflicted significant losses, Nixon called off the raids after twelve days (with a one-day pause for Christmas itself) because of the public outcry and because he thought he would now get his way. By that time the Vietnamese had virtually exhausted their supply of SAMs. Nevertheless, the Vietnamese looked at the results, and the results convinced them that they had won a triumph grand enough to justify, once the war was over, renaming an avenue in Hanoi "Duong Chien Thang B 52"—Avenue of the Victory over the B-52s.

In his last poem for Tet, the Lunar New Year holiday, before he died in 1969, Ho Chi Minh had prophesied that when the Americans were driven out of South Vietnam, the Saigon regime would collapse. The photographs in the museum show Ho's prophecy coming true in the wake of the combat with the flying machines. A month afterward, Kissinger and Le Duc Tho are seen initialing the Paris Agreement, under which Nixon pulled the remaining American combat forces out of the South. There is a photograph of the flag coming down at the headquarters of the United States Military Assistance Command Vietnam in Saigon. Two years later the final offensive that Nixon sought to avert began and an exhibit dated April 30, 1975, displays the mementos of the end: a fragment of the gate from Thieu's palace in Saigon; a picture of the last president of South Vietnam, Gen. Duong Van Minh, once also a favorite of the Americans, who took over the presidency a couple of days before the fall, his head bowed; a blown-up reproduction of his handwritten declaration of unconditional surrender; the actual T-54 tank that broke open the gate—Tank No. 843 of the 203rd Armored Brigade.

The Army Museum memorializes the country's modern war for independence. The Historical Museum in Hanoi tells why that thirty-year ordeal was fought. One has to go there to understand what has shaped the Vietnamese, what for them is past and present and to come: China. The first of the great Chinese dynasties, the Han, was also the first to invade Vietnam, in III B.C., conquering the Red River delta and imposing more than a millennium of Chinese colonization. The citadel of the ancient Vietnamese dynasty the Chinese crushed, called Co Loa, was located just ten miles from Hanoi, on the road to Noi Bai Airport. It was excavated by Vietnamese archaeologists in the 1960s and '70s, and the museum has a model of Co Loa with its triple earthen walls and moats. A big bronze drum discovered at the site had scenes of daily living depicted in rings around a sunburst design at the center— some not unlike what I saw in the modern Red River delta: people threshing rice, fishing from a boat. With the conquest by the Han, Vietnamese life—administration, architecture, dress—took on Chinese forms. Yet the forms retained a Vietnamese content. The language was written in Chinese characters; the words were Vietnamese. The exhibits depicting the repeated rebellions—of the Trung sisters from A.D. 40 to 43; of another woman, Ba Trieu, two hundred years later—convey the impression of a people who felt their identity, their sense of being Vietnamese, too keenly to have it extinguished by foreigners.

The thousand years of tension between colonization and resistance suddenly erupted in the first Battle of Bach Dang in 938, when a patriotic mandarin named Ngo Quyen destroyed a Chinese fleet and army and won Vietnam its independence. The battle took place in the mouth of the Bach Dang River on the northern edge of the delta. The museum had a reconstruction of it in a large glass case. The Chinese ships were imposing in size and bristling bow to stern with the troops of a grand army; the Vietnamese boats sallying out to attack and burn them were small. The Chinese were outsmarted. They had thought they would sail up the river and land at their convenience. But the Vietnamese had planted stakes with pointed tips in the river bottom. When the tide fell, the Chinese ships were impaled on the stakes and could not move. Thus were the mighty neutralized and rendered prey to Vietnamese spear and arrow and torch.

On a rear wall of the museum the visitor encounters a painting of an identical battle panorama in the same river mouth exactly 350 years later. The Mongols, the invincible warriors who rode out of the Gobi Desert under Genghis Khan to sweep fear through the world from Korea to Hungary, had conquered all of China and established a new dynasty there under Kublai Khan. They had already invaded Vietnam twice, in 1257 and in 1284, and the Vietnamese had acquired the distinction of twice recovering from initial disasters to defeat them at great cost and chase the survivors back to China.

As stubborn as they were ferocious, the Mongols had returned in 1287 and once more been bested. It was now 1288. Their army was attempting to sail home to China to recuperate and come back to fight another day. Tran Hung Dao, the renowned Vietnamese soldier-mandarin, remembered Ngo Quyen's trick. The Mongol ships were also impaled on pointed stakes at the ebb of the tide, and the little Vietnamese boats swarmed out to burn them with torches and flaming trees. More than four hundred ships filled with Mongol soldiery were destroyed, and the Mongols never again invaded Vietnam. There was even an exhibit of what the museum claimed were some of Tran Hung Dao's stakes, excavated from the mud of the river bottom.

The particular identity of the menace changed, but always the menace came out of China. The Vietnamese have never been able to avoid the menace because they are trapped by geography on the edge of this vast empire.

A cemetery on a hill overlooking the border village of Dong Dang bears witness to the Vietnamese that the threat is eternal. The graves on the hilltop are the resting places of soldiers who died stopping an invasion by one of the Communist emperors of twentieth-century China, Deng Xiaoping. The cemetery and the border village are a short distance beyond Lang Son, the largest town occupied by the Chinese when they invaded in February 1979.

The road from Hanoi took us three hours to drive, northeast across the delta through its crowded villages and towns, then up into the foothills, then through the mountains to the valleys and rugged hills along this section of the frontier. The closer I got to the border, the more evidence I saw of military preparedness—the headquarters compound of Military Region I with its antiaircraft radar and flak cannons; another camp with tanks lined up neatly under sheds; antitank gun positions dug into slopes where the gunners could shoot straight down a gorge at an armored column strung out along the road. After a while it became apparent that this preparedness was a purposeful show, like the thirty-five silver MiG jet fighters I had noted ostentatiously lined up along the runway on the military side of Noi Bai Airport. Vegetation had not been permitted to grow around and conceal the gun positions. The earth was kept fresh so that everyone, but especially Chinese spies, would see that Vietnam was ready.

History lay along the road too. Twenty miles south of Lang Son the road traversed a narrow pass called the Chi Lang Gate (Ai Chi Lang) because it had been the entry point—or the stopping point—for so many armies marching down from China. In 1427 the wily Le Loi ended a nine-year war against the Ming Dynasty by fighting a decisive battle here, luring a Chinese army into a massive ambush that stretched out along several miles of the road. To a foreign visitor the event occurred more than five and a half centuries ago. To the Vietnamese it was yesterday. We stopped at Ai Chi Lang because I had read about the place and wanted to look at it. I discovered a large schematic of the battle erected beside the road at the base of a peak called Ghost Mountain at the entrance to the pass. The schematic showed each of the fifty-two places in the pass where Le Loi's troops had hidden and waited.

John Kennedy and Lyndon Johnson led the United States to war in Vietnam at the beginning of the 1960s because they believed that Ho Chi Minh and his disciples were pawns of Communist China and that in stopping them the United States would prevent China from taking over the rest of Southeast Asia. The American war had hardly ended in 1975 when history reared up to mock this illusion.

After the Vietnamese invaded Cambodia in December 1978 to

overthrow the homicidal ultraleftist Pol Pot, who was being sustained by China, Deng Xiaoping decided, according to his explanation, to teach the Vietnamese a lesson. In another ironic turnabout, Deng would attempt to teach his lesson with American approval, for by this time Washington and Beijing had become allies. President Jimmy Carter and his special assistant for national security affairs, Zbigniew Brzezinski, were "playing the China card," as Brzezinski put it, in the global rivalry with the Soviet Union. Joachim Brodie Groger, the West German ambassador to Vietnam and the wit of the diplomatic community, held a different opinion tempered by the view from Hanoi: "The Chinese were playing the American card." Dang Nghiem Bai, a man with a mordant sense of humor who was the head of the North-American Affairs Department at the Foreign Ministry in Hanoi, agreed that Deng's purpose in invading was instructive. "The Chinese came to teach us a lesson—for the seventeenth time."

The Chinese did not get far, nor did they stay long on this occasion. Their regular army had not fought since another border war with India in 1962 and did badly against the local Vietnamese troops, the Frontier Guards and the regional forces, taking thousands of casualties to get to Lang Son, 11 miles by road from the border. They held Lang Son for a mere four days and Dong Dang for twenty before pulling back into their own territory in March 1979. Vietnam's regular divisions, which had been in Cambodia, were moving up to counterattack, and the Chinese apparently thought better of the matter. As they withdrew they demolished Lang Son, dynamiting most of the houses, the hospital, the high school, and other public buildings.

Although the fighting continued for years after 1979 with artillery duels and lesser incursions, the Vietnamese finished rebuilding Lang Son by 1986. There was a new three-story hospital and a new high school. The only reminders of the war I could see in the town were the pockmarks of bullets on an occasional wall. The bridge along the road between Lang Son and Dong Dang, destroyed three times in the last half century—by the retreating French colonials, by the American bombing, and by the Chinese retreating in the opposite direction from the French—has been rebuilt too.

The name of the place where the road and railroad had crossed into China just past Dong Dang—"Friendship Gate"—was only faintly visible on the map in the Lang Son office of the Service of External Relations, the Vietnamese bureaucracy responsible for dealing with foreign visitors. It had been wiped out with alcohol. The official who briefed me said the Vietnamese are nevertheless going to retain the name of Friendship Gate because it is a historical one. They are, in fact, reviving the name because to do so suits their purpose in the current phase of a pattern long established by the wars with China. Once the "aggressor to the north," the code words for China I often heard during our stay, is beaten or fought to a draw, the Vietnamese make peace.

The border-crossing point had reopened informally about the time the rebuilding of Lang Son was complete, and trade had since picked up to a level that was extremely brisk. The road and the railroad into China were scheduled to be repaired and reopened within a year. In the meantime Vietnamese traders had to walk the last few miles between Dong Dang and the crossing point along the destroyed railroad bed to avoid being blown up on mines and had to carry the goods they bought back the same way, but this was not deterring anyone. The Chinese merchants on the other side accepted Vietnamese dong and rice and other agricultural products in payment. The closer we got to Lang Son on the way up, the more often we were passed by buses, trucks, and vans filled with Vietnamese heading back south with cases of Chinese beer and cartons of umbrellas and chinaware to sell in Hanoi and other delta centers. At Lang Son I encountered several Sino-Vietnamese businessmen who had driven all the way up from Cholon, the Chinese quarter of Saigon, to explore prospects. On the return trip the traders had to run a gauntlet of three checkpoints, one at Dong Dang and two farther south, manned by customs officers and civilian and military police who were sharing in the bounty by collecting duties both official and unofficial.

The trade is important in supplying consumer goods to the

North under the new economic policy; the Vietnamese authorities are also encouraging it because it fits into their larger aim. "When you have a neighbor as big as China you can't stay enemies," one senior official explained. To create and maintain peace in centuries past, Vietnamese emperors performed a symbolic kowtow by sending tribute in gold and silver and acknowledging a fictitious suzerainty by the grand emperor in Peking. Twentieth-century Vietnam resorts to different gestures of deference; the process and objective remain the same. When I was in the North, secret high-level contacts were under way to try to satisfy Chinese pride by working out a modus vivendi over Cambodia—Vietnamese acceptance of a UN-sponsored settlement of the war there. Although the Vietnamese Communist Party had no intention of permitting a democracy movement on the Western model, the slaughter of the students in Tiananmen Square in 1989 by Deng and the Chinese old guard was widely regarded among senior officials as stupid and repugnant. The feelings were not expressed in public. Vietnam, I was told, could not afford to cause China further offense.

"China is big, but the shadow is bigger than China," Nguyen Co Thach, Vietnam's foreign minister in 1989, remarked when I saw him. He was speaking of the ability of China to project its desires upon the smaller nations of Southeast Asia. His observation applies just as cogently to how the relationship with China has molded the way the Vietnamese see the world beyond China.

The Japanese had no trouble buying priority for the unloading of their shipments at the port of Haiphong; the Vietnamese were eager for more Japanese private business and wanted credits and loans from the Japanese government because these were essential to rebuilding their economy. What the Japanese could not buy was a genuine welcome. They were suspected and resented. Some of the animosity might have resulted from the barbaric behavior of the Japanese Imperial Army in Indochina during World War II. The Vietnamese have an astonishing capacity, however, to forgive cruelty by their former enemies. The real root of the animosity seemed to lie in a perception of Japan as a new China, threatening Vietnam's independence with its economic power. "The Japanese are the worst Chinese I know," a member of the Politburo said to a European ambassador one day.

This attitude was one of the motives behind the keen desire to make peace with the United States. With the United States no longer a threat, the Vietnamese see an American diplomatic and business presence as a political counterpoise to China and an economic counterpoise to Japan. The commercial relationships being developed with South Korea, Hong Kong, Taiwan, Singapore, Thailand, and Australia are all being encouraged for their immediate benefit and for this same counterpoise effect.

Yet there is more than practical consideration behind the wish to come to terms with the former American enemy, as an American who spent some time in Vietnam could soon see. The desire went beyond the practical and into the emotional, into the realm of patterns from the past.

I was standing by the side of the road with Thang in a village on the way to Lang Son. Our driver had stopped to get a flat tire fixed. A farmer came along on a bicycle. He halted in surprise at seeing a foreigner, pointed his finger at me and asked, *"Lien Xo?* [Russian?]" I shook my head and answered, *"My,"* which means "American." The farmer smiled. *"Tot* [good]," he said with satisfaction. Thang started translating. The farmer's clothes were old and torn, most of his teeth were missing, and his hair was gray, prematurely as it turned out. "Americans are good," he said. I thanked him. "Vietnamese are good too," he said, wanting to know if I agreed. I did. "I'm a veteran," the farmer said proudly. "I fought in the South." I asked where and then remarked that the fighting in that area had been bitter. "Yes, so many bombs, so many shells, so much napalm my head turned like this," the farmer said, leaning forward and pointing at his hair. He held out his hand to me. *"Hoa binh,"* he said as we shook, then cycled off down the road. *Hoa binh* means "peace."

I encountered this lack of animosity everywhere we went in the North and kept asking for an explanation. The first offered was that the Vietnamese had never regarded the entire American people as their enemy. The American government—"the imperialists"—

had been the enemy; other Americans, particularly the antiwar protesters, had been on the Vietnamese side. This did not seem explanation enough for people like the farmer on the road to Lang Son. He had suffered dearly at the hands of Americans who had not been an abstract "imperialist" entity. One afternoon in a village near Haiphong, when Susan and I were with Tran Le Tien, our other guide-interpreter, we were received with kindness by a family who had lost a son in the South. On the way back to Hanoi I said to Tien that there had to be more to this attitude than good Americans versus bad Americans. "It's the wars with China," Tien said. I decided he was right.

Above all else, the never-ending struggle with China has imprinted the theme of sacrifice on Vietnamese culture. The words on the obelisk in the cemetery on the hill overlooking Dong Dang read *"To Quoc Ghi Cong* [The Land of Your Ancestors Will Remember Your Good Deeds]." At the top of the obelisk is a lotus flower, the Buddhist symbol of Nirvana, and at the base an urn of honor. Vietnamese who fall in battle are not referred to as Honored Dead. The words engraved at the top of each headstone read *"Liet Sy* [Martyr]." The name of the soldier is given, his date of birth, home village, home district, home province, and then the day he fell—although he did not fall. Rather, the words before the date said, he was "Sacrificed" *(Hy Sinh)*. The low white masonry tombs erected in front of the headstones were darkening with moss. Many of the little blue-and-white porcelain bowls that held sand in which to place incense sticks were cracked and broken.

For the French and the Americans the wars stopped. The Vietnamese had to go on paying the price of independence. The nineteen- and twenty- and twenty-one-year-old youths buried here died nearly four years after the last American helicopter lifted off the roof of the U.S. Embassy in Saigon. As the story at the Chi Lang Gate told, they were not the first generation of their people, nor are they likely to be the last, to die safeguarding the green of the rice paddies below this cemetery hill and the green on the distant limestone hills along the Chinese border.

. . .

Gen. Doan Khue, Vietnam's minister of defense, used to have six brothers. His mother, who is in her eighties, has two sons left, General Khue and the one brother who survived the French and American wars. A frail woman who is unable to receive visitors, she is a member of a special group of people in Vietnam. They are called "mothers of martyrs."

Mrs. Thai Thi Thinh is a mother of martyrs. She lives in a quiet section of the city. Susan and I called on her on one of our last afternoons in Hanoi. She is a diminutive lady, doll-like in wispiness, with thinning gray hair, delicate pretty features, and porcelain skin. Her hand shook a bit as she poured tea. She said she was recovering from a cough she had developed with the onset of the summer heat.

Mrs. Thinh was born in 1911 in Nghe An, the native province of Ho Chi Minh. Her father was a civil servant in the French colonial road construction bureau. When she was eighteen she married an enterprising young man who had just graduated from the University of Hanoi as a medical officer. His work took her and their family—Mrs. Thinh was to give birth to eight children—to hospitals where he was assigned in Central and North Vietnam.

She lost children for the first time at Lang Son during World War II. Her husband had been away in France on temporary assignment with Vietnamese labor troops the French had recruited. He hurried back to Vietnam when the Germans invaded in 1940 because he was worried that the sea-lanes would be closed. Her three-year-old girl and five-year-old son had become gravely ill. Her husband asked the chief French doctor at the Lang Son hospital to do everything he could. "Even the French doctor couldn't save them," Mrs. Thinh said.

In August 1945, with the end of World War II and the beginning of the Viet Minh drive for independence, Mrs. Thinh's husband joined the cause of Ho Chi Minh. He was put in charge of the health care service for Hanoi. When full-scale fighting with the French broke out in December 1946, he evacuated Mrs. Thinh and the children to the countryside, then told his wife that he had to go back into the city to care for the wounded. She never saw him again. Repeated attempts to find out what had happened to him elicited no information.

Mrs. Thinh gathered her six children, five sons and a daughter, around her. They built a house in a village near Phu Tho northwest of Hanoi, and the children went to school there. Her eldest son, a fine student, graduated from the high school and joined the combat engineers. During the battle of Dien Bien Phu in 1954 his unit was assigned to keeping open the jungle roads along which truck convoys moved with ammunition and other essential supplies for the assault troops. A dud bomb dropped by a French plane threatened to disrupt traffic at a road junction if it went off. He volunteered to defuse it. He was killed when the bomb exploded. Accounts of his death, praising his selflessness, were published in Viet Minh newspapers. One of the soldiers to whom the trucks were hauling supplies was his younger brother, fighting at Dien Bien Phu as an infantryman in the renowned 308th Division, which suffered the highest casualties of the four infantry divisions engaged. He survived the battle, to be killed not long afterward in a subsequent clash with the French while the division was advancing on Hanoi.

The French defeat allowed Mrs. Thinh to return to Hanoi in 1955. She went to work as the switchboard operator at the Institute for Sanitation Service. To help feed and clothe her four remaining children, she sewed army uniforms in her spare time. The remains of her eldest son were brought back from the jungle and buried in the municipal cemetery in Hanoi. His younger brother was buried in a memorial cemetery in the forest where he had fallen about fifty miles from the city. Mrs. Thinh visits their graves as often as she can.

A decade passed, and she and her family were once more caught up in war. In 1965, as the Saigon regime was collapsing under the onslaught of the Viet Cong guerrillas, Lyndon Johnson launched his "Rolling Thunder" bombing campaign against the North and sent the might of the U.S. Army and the Marine Corps into the South. Ho Chi Minh proclaimed a general mobilization to resist the new foreign threat, penning the sentence that is reproduced in an eighteen-karat-gold replica of his handwriting on the wall inside the entrance to his mausoleum in Hanoi: "Nothing is more precious than independence and freedom." All military-age males fit to serve were liable for conscription, regardless of what their families had endured in the French war. Mrs. Thinh's youngest son, then twenty-four years old, had graduated from a technical high school in Hanoi and was working in a factory. He was drafted and sent to the South.

In 1967 she got two letters from him that were carried back up the Ho Chi Minh Trail. He was a gunner in an antiaircraft unit fighting in the mountains of the Central Highlands. He had been cited for valor and awarded the title of "Best Shooter-Down of Planes" in his battalion. She didn't hear from him after that, but she assumed that he was all right, that it was simply too difficult for him to send letters. She did not fear she had lost him because he was such a fine athlete and she felt he would be able to take care of himself. He had run every morning, raced on the factory track team, played basketball, and after work liked to swim in Hanoi's biggest lake, the Ho Tay or West Lake. She got up from her chair and took down from the wall a glass-covered photograph of him. The photograph showed a good-looking, lithe young man dressed in civilian clothes. The picture was taken on a leave he was granted just before his unit left for the South.

In 1972 she was told that he had died in May 1968, in a battle in Cu Chi District in the rubber plantation country near Saigon. The surprise offensive at Tet, on January 31, 1968, had broken the will of the Johnson administration to prosecute the war. Lyndon Johnson had renounced any possibility of another term as president and opened negotiations. To keep pressure on the United States, the Hanoi leaders had ordered another all-out offensive that May, called the "May Tet" by Americans. Many of the May assaults were so unrealistic in military terms that they were suicidal.

Because Mrs. Thinh had parted with so much, the Minister of Labor, War Invalids, and Social Welfare came to her apartment himself at the end of 1972 to offer his sympathy and to ask if it would be convenient for the family to officially announce her son's sacrifice. Mrs. Thinh consented. The ministry and the local community authorities organized a funeral ceremony at the apartment. She was informed during the ceremony that her son had become a battlefield member of the Vietnamese Communist Party and had been awarded two high decorations, one by the regular Vietnam People's Army, or North Vietnamese Army, as the U.S. military had referred to it, and another by the Viet Cong guerrillas.

A mother of martyrs has privileges. Mrs. Thinh's apartment, a fourth-floor walkup in a building constructed in 1970, is better than most. She shares it with one of her two surviving sons, Chu Mai Loc, an accountant who is Party secretary at the Ministry of Light Industry, and his wife, who works at the same ministry. They returned a few minutes before five P.M. at the end of their workday, and the son joined in the interview while Mrs. Thinh's daughter-in-law served us glasses of sweet lemonade chilled with chopped ice.

The apartment consists of the sitting room, where Mrs. Thinh's bed was located, a bedroom for the couple, and a tiny kitchen where the daughter-in-law began rattling pans as she prepared supper—thirty-five square meters (about 125 square feet) of space (the bathroom is unconnected and shared with other tenants). The dreary green paint on the walls is a shade I saw so often that I named it "Hanoi green," and the roof had leaked almost from the day the family had moved in fifteen years before, but the view from the sitting room window is nice. The family hopes to move soon to a new forty-eight-square-meter (about 172 square feet) apartment Mrs. Thinh is being granted on the ground floor of a building still under construction in central Hanoi. It will have a bigger kitchen and a private bathroom. Mrs. Thinh was looking forward to the absence of stairs.

When she retired from her switchboard operator's job in 1966 at the age of fifty-five, she received a pension for four—for herself and the three martyrs in her family up to that time. She was then given a substantial sum of money after word came of the death of her youngest. A grandson had been in Dresden in the former East Germany for the last seven years as a mechanic in a factory producing spare parts for sewing machines. At the request of his grandmother, he was among the first Vietnamese privileged to work overseas. Mrs. Thinh receives gifts from the government on national holidays, and she hopes someday to go on one of the brief trips abroad that the government occasionally provides mothers of martyrs in January or February as winter vacations. She does not seem to take her privileges for granted. "We try to be self-sufficient," she said.

Despite her physical fragility, Mrs. Thinh remains a strong woman. She is cheerful and uncomplaining, noting how lucky she is to have three places to live in Hanoi; she often goes to stay for a few days at the apartment of her other surviving son, a forestry expert, or with her daughter's family. The sadness she does carry has pride in it. She opened an album on the low table around which we were sitting and showed us photographs of herself wearing the medals of the four national orders she had been awarded, three for the French war, one for the American.

What troubles her most is her inability to learn what happened to her husband and to find the remains of her youngest son and give them proper burial. The son with whom Mrs. Thinh lives, Chu Mai Loc, went down to Cu Chi District right after the collapse of the Saigon regime in 1975 to try to bring home his brother's remains. He was told there wasn't a chance of discovering a trace, that the fighting in which his brother had died had been so intense the entire unit had been annihilated. Because such circumstances of combat, or confusion and lack of records, were typical, the hundreds of thousands of other Vietnamese families with relatives missing in action have no choice but to live with a similar burden.

In December 1976, after the formal reunification of Vietnam, Mrs. Thinh traveled to the South with other mothers of martyrs on one of the first trains to run over the rebuilt tracks of the old Hanoi–Saigon railroad. She was given a tour of the tunnel complex at Cu Chi that had been a famed guerrilla base and was shown a map illustrating the position of her son's antiaircraft unit at the time of the 1968 battle. "When I saw that, I couldn't keep myself from bursting out in tears," she said calmly now. She shook hands when we left. "Thank you for calling on me on such a hot day," she said.

Saigon
and the
South

For me the memories began at 10,000 feet over the Central Highlands of the South. In the years that were coming back to me, the pilot would have been worried about ground fire and stayed high until he was right over Saigon, then banked the plane down sharply for the runway at Tan Son Nhut. The pilot of the twin-engine Tupolev jet of Hang Khong Viet Nam, the Vietnamese national airline, bringing us and other morning travelers down from Hanoi, had been one of the victors, and he had no such memories and no such worries. He started a gradual descent while we were still far north of the city. Soon he was low enough for me to look out the window and recognize the rain-forested peaks, the wide plateaus, the serpentine valleys where entire divisions of North Vietnamese Army troops had concealed themselves under the canopy of sixty-foot-high teak and mahogany trees. The sight of that familiar dark green wildness of the Highlands had me back on a narrow mountain trail on a forbidden cross-border trek into Laos in 1963 with a Special Forces team from Dak Pek, the outpost farthest north of Kontum; back in the dust and the fear and the mad killing of Landing Zone X-Ray in the valley of the Drang River two years later, when the men of the Air Cav fought their first big battle with an enemy as brave as they were; back in the somberness of the American military advisors' compound at Pleiku in 1972, when I returned to Vietnam to do research for my book after John Vann died, to interview those who had fought his last fight with him, knowing that the end was coming soon.

The war in Vietnam was the war from which I could never get away. I first walked down a plane ramp at Saigon's Tan Son Nhut

Airport on a humid night in April 1962, worried that the Vietnamese passport control officers might not accept the journalist's visa I had hastily obtained at the South Vietnamese consulate in Hong Kong. I was twenty-five, just done with college and three years in the Army to fulfill my military service, on my first assignment as a novice reporter for a news agency, United Press International. I believed in what my country was doing in Vietnam. Like the rest of my generation, I was a child of the Cold War, with an unquestioning faith in all the tenets of the American ideology of the period. In my case the faith was undoubtedly reinforced by gratitude to an American society that practiced the social democracy it preached. My father was a hardscrabble dairy farmer, my mother an Irish immigrant who had worked as a housekeeper until her marriage, and yet I had been taken into Harvard on a scholarship and given the best education the country had to offer. I could not imagine that a nation that behaved so generously toward its own could do evil in its mission to save the world from Communism.

I was convinced that this was the right war in the right place. There was an international Communist conspiracy. If we did not win here, we would face a wave of Communist-inspired wars of national liberation throughout the underdeveloped world that would undermine the beneficial order we had so painstakingly established after our victory over Nazi Germany and Imperial Japan in World War II. To me, the domino theory was not just a theory; if South Vietnam fell, the "Sino-Soviet bloc," as the Army security clearance forms referred to our opponents, would seize the rest of Southeast Asia and then move on toward Japan.

In one of the saddest of the misplaced hopes of the war, Ho Chi Minh thought that we Americans were different from the French, that before it was too late we would prove wise enough to realize these fears were illusions. Ho made his prediction about us to a Polish diplomat in Hanoi one day in the fall of 1963, when the names of the American dead that were to number 58,183 on the black granite wall of the Vietnam Memorial were still fewer than 200. "Neither you nor I knows the Americans well," Ho said to his Polish visitor, "but what we do know of them, what we have read and heard about them, suggests that they are more practical and clear-sighted than other capitalist nations. They will not pour their resources into Vietnam endlessly. One day they will take pencil in hand and begin figuring. Once they really begin to analyze our ideas seriously, they will come to the conclusion that it is possible and even worthwhile to live in peace with us. Weariness, disappointment, the knowledge that they cannot achieve the goal which the French pursued to their own discredit will lead to a new sobriety, new feelings and emotions."

We *were* different from the French. We were far more powerful; thus we would cause far greater destruction and loss of life. Otherwise we Americans, who considered ourselves the exceptions to history, showed ourselves as fallible as the rest of humanity; we could do evil as easily as we could do good. We were all too humanly arrogant in the hubris of our moment in the sun. It was beyond us to put pencil to paper and understand that we were pursuing fantasies that would bring an immense tragedy on ourselves as well as on the Vietnamese and other peoples of Indochina.

There was, in fact, no international Communist conspiracy and no "Sino-Soviet bloc." The Communist world of the 1960s was a splintered world. The Chinese and the Soviets had openly despised each other for years. We had ignored the implications of their feud because, in our pursuit of dominion, it suited us to pretend that our enemies were one. But guerrilla wars could not be spread like bacteria, and countries were not dominos. They were living entities with national leaders who pursued their own agendas. The Vietnamese were an example. They had become Communists as an accident of French domestic politics, because only the far left in France had supported independence for the colonies. They had never been a threat to the United States. They simply wanted us to go home, and they would not cease to resist, no matter what the cost to us and to them, until we did.

It took me five years to understand that. Looking back, my first two years covering the war John Kennedy had decided to fight—in the delusion that he could put strength into the Saigon government with military advisors and Special Forces teams, helicopter companies, and fighter-bomber pilots—were a necessary lesson in skepticism. Those years were the beginning of what we would later call "the credibility gap."

Paul Harkins, the commanding general in Saigon, assured us we were winning. The advisors in the field said we were losing, that the Saigon regime's army, known as the Army of the Republic of Vietnam, or ARVN, wouldn't fight because its leadership was too incompetent or too venal or both. The most fearless and brilliant of the advisors was an articulate lieutenant colonel with a Virginia twang named John Paul Vann. I met him on my first helicopter assault in the Mekong delta a couple of months after arriving in 1962. He was destined to become America's Lawrence of Arabia in Vietnam. He helped me most during those first two years because, natural leader of men in war that he was, he could best explain what we youngsters were seeing for ourselves when we climbed into the helicopters in the cool of the breaking dawn and marched with the battalions through the heat of the delta days.

We tried to write the truth and were denounced for it by Harkins and those on high who shared his mirage. None of us wanted the United States to get out of Vietnam. We didn't know then that there was no way to win the war. We thought that if we wrote of impending defeat, the Joint Chiefs of Staff, the president—someone up there who mattered—would take action to change our policy and win. We also didn't understand yet that arrogance had rendered the American system witless, that the men in charge had made up their minds in advance and listened only to themselves. When I left Saigon in 1964 to get a job on *The New York Times,* Vann's prophecy was coming true; the Viet Cong guerrillas were well on their way to victory. (Viet Cong is an American-invented abbreviation for "Vietnamese Communists.")

The *Times* sent me back to Vietnam in August 1965, and for a year—the first year of the big American war that Lyndon Johnson decided to fight to prevent a Communist takeover of the South—I watched the United States blast and burn this country we were supposedly trying to save. Yet not until 1967, from the distance of the Pentagon correspondent's job in Washington and with the emotional wrenching of this third year of the war behind me, was I able to see the futility of our doomed venture. In retrospect a terrible inevitability seems to have been at work, as if the men who ran the United States, because of their flawed image of themselves, could have acted in no other way than they did. Lyndon Johnson was unable to endure the shame of a Viet Cong victory, and the war he magnified to prevent that victory destroyed him. His successor, Richard Nixon, refused to walk away from Johnson's mistake, saying he would not become the first American president to lose a war. He pursued victory by other means until the war destroyed him too in the Watergate scandals that the siege mentality of the war led him into, and by then the unwinnable war had been lost.

In June 1972, the man I had met during my first assault in the Mekong Delta a decade earlier was killed in a helicopter crash right after halting a North Vietnamese Army offensive in a dramatic battle at Kontum in the Highlands. During the intervening years I had never sought to escape recording the war in Vietnam or its repercussions in the United States. As tragic as the major event of my generation might be, as a reporter I felt fortunate to have been present. In 1971 I had had the privilege of obtaining the Pentagon Papers, the official secret archive of the war, for the *Times,* and by now I wanted to leave behind something more permanent than another newspaper or magazine article.

Like the other reporters who had known Vann at the beginning, I had long since parted with him over the war to which he had remained faithful. I went to his funeral because, in spite of our differences, I still considered him a friend. Walking into the chapel at Arlington National Cemetery was like entering an eerie class reunion. The chapel was filled with the small participants like me as well as the leading figures of the conflict whom Vann had encountered in his extraordinary career. Gen. William Westmoreland, who had been the commander in chief at the war's height, was his chief pallbearer. This was *the* funeral of the war. There would never be another like it because there was only one John Vann, who, by the time of his death, had become the personification of the American venture in Vietnam. If I wrote a book that told his story, I could tell the story of the war, and so I set off on an undertaking I thought would take three or four years at most. It was sixteen years until the book's publication in the fall of 1988. With the book done, I could finally return to a Vietnam at peace.

In 1965 Saigon's Tan Son Nhut Airport had been busier than Chicago's O'Hare. One waited forty-five minutes to take off, strung out in a bizarre gaggle that had a Pan American jetliner bound for Hong Kong behind a propeller-driven A-1 "Skyraider" laden with bombs and shiny aluminum canisters of napalm for some unfortunate hamlet in the countryside. Now, of course, the mad bustle was gone. Our plane from Hanoi was probably the only aircraft, including the occasional military flight, to land in an hour, and it landed at the old destination with a different name—Ho Chi Minh City, as Saigon and its environs were renamed after 1975. (In the relaxation of *doi moi*, however, people were starting to call the city Saigon again.) My journey to the North had been a voyage of discovery; almost everything I had encountered there had been new. In the South I was beginning another journey, a voyage of rediscovery through the kaleidoscope of the past and the emotions it aroused. As was to be the case wherever I went through a changed but familiar land, something inevitably called the past to mind.

At Tan Son Nhut it was the archaeology of our American empire—rows of half-moon-shaped concrete shelters, erected at considerable expense, to safeguard U.S. warplanes from Communist mortar and rocket attacks. The shelters were empty, and weeds were growing among them. On the drive into the city it was the coils of rusting concertina wire on top of the compound walls that had protected the homes of former Saigon government officials and buildings rented to Americans. The Vietnamese who lived in them now apparently found the barbed wire a deterrent to burglars and, as with much else the Americans had left behind, no one had gotten around to removing it.

The street signs along the main avenue from the airport said

"Nguyen Van Troi" where before they had said "Cach Mang," but the new name evoked a memory too. At a small bridge about halfway into town, Nguyen Van Troi, a twenty-four-year-old electrician, had tried to set off a bomb under a car carrying Robert McNamara, secretary of defense during the Kennedy and Johnson administrations, on one of McNamara's periodic visits to assess the war. Nguyen Van Troi had died before a firing squad in Saigon's Chi Hoa Prison in 1964 shouting "Long live Ho Chi Minh."

We checked into the Rex, scene of the "Five O'Clock Follies" during the war, the derisive nickname the press corps had coined for the military briefing each afternoon. Thanks to the determination of its director, Dao Huu Loan, an enterprising Northerner who had emigrated to the South in 1975, to turn it into the best hotel in town, the Rex had come a long way from its days as a propaganda mill downstairs and a bachelor officers' quarters on the upper floors. A marble lobby had replaced the mundane side entrance that once led to the offices of JUSPAO, or Joint U.S. Public Affairs Office. The ground floor at the front of the hotel where the briefings were held had become a bar and an expanse of souvenir shops, but I could still see the rows of seats filled with reporters and the podium where the briefing officer had stood to announce how many sorties had been flown, how many "structures" had been destroyed, how many "contacts" had been made with the enemy.

Nixon's strategy to win the war in its final years had been to gain public support in the United States by gradually withdrawing American troops, while shifting the burden of the fighting in Vietnam to the Saigon regime's forces. He had called his policy "Vietnamization." Ironically, Saigon was being "Vietnamized" because his policy had failed. The Rex was an example of what was happening to the city. For the first time since the French seized permanent control in 1861, Saigon was becoming a Vietnamese place. The Vietnamese really were in charge now, and they were gradually putting to their own use what the French and Americans had built and left behind. In the process the past could sometimes be difficult to find even if one searched for it consciously.

During the war everyone had known the location of the grand emporium of American civilization, the main PX in Cholon, the Chinese section of the city. Susan had bought the ornaments for our first Christmas tree there on a steamy day in August 1965. The air-conditioning had been turned up high, and Bing Crosby was singing "White Christmas" over the stereo system. "Buy them now, lady," a Pfc. serving as salesclerk had admonished her when he spotted her looking at the ornaments. "They'll be gone in a week." Twenty-four years later we met an older Chinese businessman who remembered where the PX had been and drew a sketch of the intersection. We still had trouble finding it. Numerous people on nearby streets had no recollection.

Thang and I finally discovered it by peering over the gate of an abandoned compound. The Vietnamese had turned the site into a dump for the scrap they sell to dealers from Southeast Asian neighbors like Singapore and the Philippines. The yard in front was filled with the carcasses of trucks and other cast-off military vehicles, piles of worn-out tires, and rusted shipping containers with "U.S. Army" still visible in white on the weathered green paint. The whitewashed stucco buildings behind, once beckoning with cornucopias of Scotch whisky and filter cigarettes, hi-fis and television sets, room air conditioners, lipstick and hair spray to tempt Vietnamese women, were abandoned and gray with moss.

Then, at a moment when one least expected it, the past was there. At the Ho Chi Minh City Arts and Literature Association the conversation moved from trying to stem the showing of porno-graphic and violent videotapes in a city where there were an estimated 20,000 VCRs, to the travails of self-sufficiency brought on by *doi moi*. Parked in the courtyard was a ten-wheel Soviet military truck, freshly painted in bright yellow but otherwise old enough to have come down the Ho Chi Minh Trail, that the association had bought in a so far money-losing enterprise to haul logs to sawmills from the rain forests of Tay Ninh. The vice-chairman, a writer of short stories named Vien Phuong, mentioned that the association's headquarters had previously belonged to the mother-in-law of General Nguyen Van Thieu, the last American strongman. Would we like to see a safe in which he had found two million Saigon government piastres? Mr. Phuong asked.

He had discovered the safe in a bedroom he was currently using as an office after the house had been seized in 1975 and had sent for a welder to cut it open with an acetylene torch. Mr. Phuong said he had used the cash to support fellow writers during the months immediately following the fall of Saigon because the former government's currency, although worthless outside the country, had remained legal tender with considerable purchasing power for quite a while. There were five more safes in the house, but Mr. Phuong had found them already opened and cleaned out by Thieu's mother-in-law before she fled. One still stood bizarrely on a stair landing, somehow dragged there in the panic at the end, the symbol of a society so corrupt that it had finally collapsed of its own moral emptiness.

The Vietnamese had bestowed the best-known foreign residence in the city on their Soviet benefactors. The Russian consul general slept in the two-story villa where Ellsworth Bunker, the longest-serving U.S. ambassador in Saigon, had lived from 1967 to 1973. Like his Vietnamese hosts, the consul general had not taken the trouble to remove the accoutrements of the past, and so he had a house that might have been better appreciated by a Russian diplomat in Afghanistan—a spiked grille along the top of the front compound wall, floodlights, a reinforced concrete tower where Marine guards in battle gear had once crouched when the Viet Cong had attempted a surprise attack through the old Mac Dinh Chi cemetery at the end of the street.

The tombstones the guerrillas hid behind were gone because of a postwar policy of turning urban cemeteries into parks. The remains of the two most famous occupants of the cemetery, Ngo Dinh Diem, the Catholic mandarin installed in power by the United States in 1954 and then overthrown and assassinated in an American-sponsored coup in 1963 after he had become a liability, and those of his brother and virtual coruler, Ngo Dinh Nhu, assassinated with him, were not claimed by relatives, and so were cremated and placed with other unclaimed remains in a mausoleum north of the city. Now rock bands played on weekend nights on the open-air stage in the park. There was an outdoor coffee shop. A park guard in a blue uniform blew a whistle at two young people riding a forbidden bicycle along one of the shrub-lined walks.

General Westmoreland's house had been less fortunate in its heir. The Ho Chi Minh City branch of the Vietnamese Women's Federation was doing nothing to keep the place up. A traditional colonial mansion in ochre with white trim and louvered green shutters, the house had been elegant, particularly during the early 1960s in the time of Westmoreland's predecessor as commander in chief, General Harkins, when the war had still been a countryside affair that did not seem to threaten the city. General Harkins had occasionally invited reporters to the house to meet some distinguished visitor from Washington. An Army sergeant in starched khakis who served as the butler would greet us under the covered doorway off the circular drive. The Vietnamese servants had worn white uniforms.

Now a sign on the street outside, in front of a cage where a sentry had stood, advertised bus tours to the seaside resort of Vung Tau and to Da Lat in the mountains—the equivalent for the Women's Federation of the log-hauling enterprise launched by the Arts and Literature Association. Four tour buses were parked inside the walled grounds where jeeps and staff cars and General Westmoreland's black Chrysler Imperial had come and gone. Radio aerials lingered on the red tile roof, no longer communicating with anyone.

Other former American buildings had been placed on hold toward the hoped-for day when Washington would end its economic embargo and establish diplomatic relations. The buildings were being kept under official or semiofficial ownership so that they could easily be vacated. I had already noticed the pattern in Hanoi. The villa there that had been the U.S. Consulate during the French years was awaiting possible conversion into the first U.S. Embassy in Vietnam's national capital. In the meantime it was serving as a headquarters for the Fatherland Front, the government-controlled political and civic organization to encourage national unity.

The fortresslike building of seven stories with a helicopter pad on the roof that had been the U.S. Embassy in Saigon was temporarily serving as offices for Vietnam's petroleum bureaucracy until it could be reopened as the first U.S. Consulate in Ho Chi Minh City. The consulate would need more office space than the embassy in Hanoi. It would have to handle the concerns of the largest Vietnamese community overseas, the more than a million Vietnamese who at present live in the United States, a community constantly growing because of immigration, illegally as "boat people" and legally through the Orderly Departure Program run by both governments. Virtually all are from the South, the largest number from the Saigon-Cholon area, and most have relatives in Vietnam. Since the reformers within the Party gained the upper hand in 1986, thousands have begun to return each year for family visits during Tet and to explore business opportunities.

The property of the losers on the Vietnamese side was another matter. During the war one of the most closely watched streets in the city was a short one in Cholon called Ngo Quyen, where Gen. Cao Van Vien, chief of the Saigon government's Joint General Staff, lived in three adjacent houses with his family, aides, and guards. An area across the street was cleared out for his helicopter to land on. General Vien fled to the United States a few days before the end in 1975. His three houses and the helicopter pad were initially seized and turned into the headquarters for a supply unit, and then, as the Vietnamese Army began demobilizing in the 1980s, given to the unit's officers. Three retired senior colonels of the unit got the three houses. The helicopter pad went to lesser-ranking officers, who managed to build enough new apartments on it to shelter twenty-one families with shops in front to boot.

One of the three houses came with a garden. The retired colonel to whom it was given, Tran Vu Hoa, a sixty-two-year-old native of Hanoi who had spent fifteen years of the American war in the South after being sent down at the beginning in 1960, converted the garden into a café to supplement his pension. The lights of such "garden cafés" could be seen all over the city at night as every family fortunate enough to have extra space tried to turn it into money.

A genial man who said he had fought for the independence of Vietnam and friendship between the American and Vietnamese peoples, Colonel Hoa invited us inside to see the house. His wife was also retired from service during the war as an official in the Ministry of Transportation. The Hoas shared their house with one unmarried daughter, three married daughters, their husbands, and six grandchildren. In addition, Mrs. Hoa kept six cats. General Vien had been helpful to me during the war because he was an affable man and, in a contradiction that was common to the ARVN officer corps, could be perceptive and honest in private about military matters. The last time Susan and I had been to the house had been for dinner with him and his wife. It had not been crowded then.

At another house in Cholon, the offices of a small government-backed import-export firm, clerks sat and typed where I had once talked of other things. The house had been the home of an ARVN officer who was my best news source during my first two years in the country and who became one of my closest Vietnamese friends. At night in the final traumatic months of the Diem regime in 1963, I would take one of the rattletrap little yellow-and-blue Renault taxicabs that then coursed the city to some spot three or four blocks away, walk slowly in the shadows along the opposite side of the street to make sure the house was not under surveillance, then dart across. At the last minute my friend's bodyguards would throw open the gate of the courtyard and then shut it behind me.

One night while we were talking inside, the bodyguards noticed a car they thought suspicious go past the house several times. Ngo Dinh Nhu, Diem's brother, and his wife, Madame Nhu, had drawn up an assassination list, and the American correspondents were said to be on it. My friend refused to let me leave by myself. He insisted on taking me out in the back of his old Peugeot staff car—I crouching down below the window, he sitting on the seat with a pistol beside him, the driver, who was adept at losing tails, up front with a carbine slung across his lap. They dropped me off at a marketplace where I could dash away down one of the labyrinth of alleys.

As the American-sponsored coup against Diem and his family approached, my boss in Tokyo, the chief of United Press International for Asia, decided that David Halberstam, then Saigon correspondent for the *Times*, and I had become emotionally overwrought in reporting that a coup was imminent. He ordered me to fly to Tokyo for a week's rest, on pain of being fired if I refused. I asked my friend to alert me if the coup was about to occur before my scheduled return so that I could rush right back.

In the last days he was under orders confining him to garrison, but he took the risk of calling his eldest son to his office and had him carry the prearranged signal to Halberstam: "Please buy me two bottles of whiskey at the PX." I didn't get back until the day after the coup started because a careless deskman in Tokyo failed to pass me a telegram containing the follow-up warning I had also prearranged with Halberstam and Ray Herndon, another UPI reporter who was filling in for me—"Please buy me two Geisha dolls, Kyoto-style." But at least Halberstam and Herndon were forewarned and my Vietnamese friend helped me make up for my tardiness by telling me how Diem and Nhu had been assassinated. (Duong Van Minh and the other generals who staged the coup were claiming that Diem, a devout Catholic, had committed suicide.)

In later years my friend became a cabinet minister under Thieu and prospered. The Peugeot was replaced by a new black Mercedes-Benz. The house doubled in size into a fancy dwelling with more servants and a lot of air conditioners. I never asked him how he made his money, and he never objected to what I wrote about the war. After John Vann was killed in 1972 I needed a visa to return to South Vietnam to do research for the book, but as a consequence of having obtained the Pentagon Papers the previous year, I was hardly welcome. My friend lobbied hard for me to be granted the visa. It didn't matter that what I would write would not favor his cause; what counted for him was the friendship. When the end approached in the spring of 1975, I was recuperating from an auto accident and couldn't go to Saigon to cover the final act and help him escape. I wrote and telegraphed him to get out as fast as he could. He managed to wrangle seats for himself and his family on a plane a few days before the tanks arrived. Susan and I became their sponsors in the United States.

The "Vietnamizing" of the city had also gone forward in the renaming of streets. Most of the renaming, like that of the thoroughfare from the airport for Nguyen Van Troi, had been done simply to honor Communist martyrs, but in other instances there had been a deliberate attempt to wipe away the shame of the colonial past. A main crosstown street in pre-1975 Saigon was called Phan Thanh Gian, for a nineteenth-century mandarin who poisoned himself to apologize to the nation after being pressed into ceding the first Vietnamese territory to the French—Saigon and the Mekong Delta. In the catechism of the Vietnamese Communist nationalists, suicide did not excuse handing over part of the motherland to a foreign conqueror; Phan Thanh Gian should have refused and died resisting. And so history had been brought full circle by expunging his name and renaming the street for the triumph that drove the French from Vietnam—Dien Bien Phu.

Louis Pasteur, the French chemist and father of bacteriology who remained an icon to older Vietnamese physicians, was still too great a reminder of the colonial period to be given a reprieve for his good works. Pasteur Street was now called Nguyen Thi Minh Khai for the fiery daughter of a mandarin family who became the most famous woman martyr of the Vietnamese Communist cause, executed by a French firing squad at Hoc Mon near Saigon in 1941. The original U.S. Military Assistance Command Vietnam headquarters had been located on Pasteur Street. The headquarters had been astir with activity and the sense of momentous decisions being made within. A large flag had flown from the pole in front of the main building; the military policemen at the gate would snap to attention and salute the sedans with the white stars of the generals displayed on red plates. The Vietnamese Postal and Telecommunications Service had taken over the main building. The flagpole was empty. The guardroom behind the gate where the MPs had stood had been converted into a shop selling push-button phones.

Renaming the city's main street was a problem for the new rulers. Until 1954 it bore the name Catinat. Ngo Dinh Diem, Washington's first strongman, then gave it a perfectly good Vietnamese name, Tu Do, which means "freedom." The name could not be allowed to stand after 1975; it was too evocative of the American era, of Diem, who had killed thousands of ex–Viet Minh, Communists and non-Communists alike, and imprisoned tens of thousands of others in a white terror in the late 1950s, and of the generals like Nguyen Van Thieu who had followed him. The victors therefore renamed the street Dong Khoi ("uprising"). When Diem changed Catinat's name to Tu Do, the Saigonese continued to call it Catinat. Not until the late 1960s, when Diem was long dead, did the younger people begin to call it Tu Do. Now only out-of-towners call the street Dong Khoi.

As in the renaming of Phan Thanh Gian Street, history had also come full circle at the former Joint General Staff headquarters near Tan Son Nhut. The handsome compound was built by the French generals as a military command center for all of Indochina. The Saigon generals, who sided with the colonizer and served as French lieutenants during the first war for independence, sat there uneasily during the American years in the hope that they had found a second protector. Now the real Vietnamese, the Vietnamese whom no one of any consequence in Saigon knew much about during the war because they were in the jungle, issue orders there.

Lt. Gen. Nguyen Thoi Bung, commander of the 7th Military Region, which encompasses Ho Chi Minh City and the arc of provinces around it, is not a polished man. He came from a village near Tay Ninh northwest of the city. During the French war he worked his way up from the ranks in the Viet Minh, regrouped to the North after the Geneva Agreements of 1954, and acquired an education in the military. He is a proud man. After marching back down the Ho Chi Minh Trail in the early 1960s, he led regiments in the first and most famous Viet Cong division to be formed in the South, the 9th, ending the American war as division commander. "I was always an operational commander," he said, making the point that his performance in combat exempted him from having to take an assignment as a political officer.

Our interview took place on the second floor of the compound's principal three-story building, where the French and then Saigon high commands had held sway. The second floor was the floor most familiar to me because after every coup d'état the winning Saigon generals would hold a press conference there and announce fresh hopes that soon expired. General Bung said he keeps an office and receives guests in this building, but that when he has serious military business he conducts it elsewhere. Did he mean in the former Joint Operations Center across the parade ground? I asked. In the American era the term "joint" had meant combined air, land, and sea operations, but General Bung interpreted the translation as meaning collaboration with foreigners. "I don't have joint operations," he said with a frown, but otherwise the answer was yes, he uses the same place to control military operations in the region.

"I have something to show you," he said as the interview concluded. He led Susan and me downstairs and opened the door to a ghostly time capsule, the main conference room of the Saigon generals, preserved as the victors had found it in April 1975. The arrows on the acetate-covered maps lining the walls indicated, with the neatness the ARVN officers had learned during their stints at the U.S. Army Command and General Staff College at Fort Leavenworth, Kansas, the positions of Viet Cong and North Vietnamese Army units at the beginning of the last Communist offensive in March 1975. "They were correct about where my division was located," General Bung said. But the arrows also revealed that the Saigon generals had not known where the main attack would come.

Gray Naugahyde chairs were drawn up around a table in the center, waiting for the briefing officer to step up with his pointer and begin. The only indications of the passage of time were cobwebs in the corners and dust gathering on the table and chairs.

The only indication that this room had changed hands in defeat was a single bullet hole through a map on a wall near the door. One could almost hear the men who had sat here talk of high strategy and maneuver, and if one had known them one knew that neither they nor their army had believed in themselves. At the climax most of those who could get away had fled. "I haven't been in here for three or four years," General Bung said, but it was not difficult to understand why he preserved the place. The room was both a trophy and a proof to him and others like him that they had finally fought their way out of the jungle and won Saigon.

It was a Sunday morning in July, and we were standing in the living room of what used to be the British ambassador's residence in Saigon at 261 Dien Bien Phu. Thang, Tien, Ambassador Vu Hac Bong, the chief of the Ho Chi Minh City Service of External Relations, two officials from his press office, and an interpreter we had not met before, whose English was unusually fluent, were there too. We were awaiting the arrival of Nguyen Van Linh, general secretary of the Vietnamese Communist Party, a man who had survived twelve years of French prisons, thirty years of war and manhunts in the South, and a decade of internecine political struggle after the Communist victory in 1975 to ultimately start his country down a new path amidst the new turmoil of peace.

There was no customary roar of engines from the security escort cars when Mr. Linh did arrive. Such emblems of status were not his style, and having lived so much of his life with danger he did not seem concerned about it. When he was chosen general secretary in 1986, he had dismissed the security escorts of his predecessor, Le Duan. The car that pulled into the driveway was a modest one called a Lada, the Soviet version of a Fiat, with Mr. Linh in the back and a single bodyguard up front beside the driver.

In Hanoi Vietnamese leaders of Mr. Linh's generation, men in their seventies, normally dressed in one of two ways for semiformal occasions like an interview: a short-sleeved blouse and slacks in extremely hot weather, or a high-collar tunic like the one Ho had worn, often referred to as a "Mao jacket" in the West because the

Chinese leader had also favored it. They usually did not wear the preferred dress of younger officials, a safari shirt and slacks, which the Vietnamese called *bo ky gia*, literally "correspondent's suit," for the American television correspondents who had introduced it to the country. The choice had to do with outlook rather than age. Despite his national office, Mr. Linh spent more time in Saigon than he did in Hanoi, and on this Sunday morning he wore a *bo ky gia* neatly cut of gray-green cotton.

Until he emerged from the jungle in 1975, little was known of Nguyen Van Linh, and a decade and a half afterward little is still known of him outside of Vietnam. Although he was an important Viet Minh figure in the South during the French war and one of the handful of ranking Communist leaders there throughout the American conflict, the United States Information Service noted in a biographical sketch published as late as April 1973 that there was "insufficient information available from which to construct a proper profile" of him. Strangely enough, the profile that was published, based on CIA and military intelligence reports, identified him as Nguyen Van Cuc, his real name at birth in Hanoi on July 1, 1915, but lacked the early alias, Nguyen Van Linh, that he had long since adopted as his name. The number of lesser *noms de guerre* Mr. Linh employed over the years to confuse the intelligence services of France and America—Muoi, Muoi Cuc, Muoi Ut, Buu Cuc, Rau, Bay—understandably made it difficult to determine precisely who he was.

He was always different. Ho Chi Minh and most of the original generation of revolutionaries who followed him—like Pham Van Dong, prime minister of the North for many years, who polished Linh's French when they were prisonmates on the penal island of Poulo Condore off the coast southeast of Saigon during the 1930s—were from mandarin families with nationalist sympathies. Mr. Linh was not. "My parents were well-paid civil servants of the French administration," he said. His father was a professor in a lycée in Hanoi. Linh does not recall the subject his father taught because his father died when he was eight and he went to live with an uncle in Haiphong who was a minor official in the colonial legal system. The uncle enrolled him in a lycée there for a proper French education.

The nationalist sentiment spreading among young Vietnamese caught him just the same. He joined a clandestine youth organization, and in 1929, at the age of fourteen, he was arrested with two classmates while distributing anti-French leaflets. He got eighteen months in jail. The following year a series of uprisings in the North frightened the colonial authorities. Special tribunals were set up with the power to condemn dissidents to the guillotine or impose life imprisonment. Although French law said that Linh should be tried as a juvenile, he was taken before a tribunal at the end of the eighteen months and resentenced as an adult to ten years on Poulo Condore.

Victor Hugo and *Les Misérables,* not Karl Marx and *Das Kapital,* pointed him toward Communism. He had given no thought to social issues until one day not long before his arrest. Several older members of the clandestine youth organization, whom he later discovered were already versed in Communist beliefs, posed a question to him: After they had driven the foreigner from the country, would he be satisfied to live in a Vietnam ridden by the social injustice he could see around him? "At this moment I had started reading *Les Misérables* and the image of Jean Valjean was very striking to me—a poor man, so poor he had to beg for his daily bread," Mr. Linh said in his expressive way, smiling, frowning, gesturing with his small hands as he spoke, switching from Vietnamese to French, to the consternation of the interpreter. He had also read a novel by Hector Malot, another nineteenth-century French romanticist, about an orphan boy named Rémi. "He had to travel with a circus all over Europe to earn his living." But Victor Hugo was the decisive influence on him, and *Les Misérables* remains his favorite novel. "It touched the strings of my heart very directly—I was very moved," Mr. Linh said. So he gave his answer: "I could not be satisfied with a society where there is an enormous gap between rich and poor." Then he would have to struggle for two goals, the older students said: national independence and social revolution.

Penal servitude on Poulo Condore (the island was renamed Con Dao after 1975), a "University of the Revolution," as Mr. Linh remarked in a common but apt Vietnamese description of the French prison system, furthered his political education. Pham Van Dong, seven years older and a founding member of the Vietnamese Communist Party, was more than Linh's "professeur de français" on the island. He was also one of Linh's instructors in Marxism-Leninism. When Linh was released in 1936 in an amnesty by the Popular Front government in France, he joined the Party and went to work in Haiphong organizing cells among laborers. He did not stay free for long. The outbreak of World War II returned Indochina to normalcy—repression. The French police picked him up in Vinh in Central Vietnam, where he had been dispatched to try to rescue a newly shattered Party apparatus, and shipped him back to Poulo Condore.

The reason Mr. Linh remained a twilight figure until 1975 was simple: He never left the South. Liberation from Poulo Condore in 1945, when Japan, which had conquered Indochina, surrendered and the first war for Vietnamese independence broke out, meant for him thirty years of never having a safe place to sleep. Others fought the French in the South and regrouped to the North after the Geneva Agreements of 1954. Mr. Linh was assigned to be one of the "stay-behinds," as the CIA labeled them, who were kept in the South to lead a political struggle for the 1956 all-Vietnam election that had been provided for at Geneva, an election that was never to take place. He became the leading "stay-behind," the ranking Communist in South Vietnam, when Le Duan, another of Mr. Linh's prisonmates on Poulo Condore, was summoned to the North in 1956 and Mr. Linh replaced him as Party secretary for the South.

The Vietnamese have a special term for those like Mr. Linh who stayed in 1954. They are known as "winter cadres" because they survived the winter of the terror Diem and the CIA launched to track them down. The trials of the American war that was to follow were grim, and Mr. Linh recalled them vividly. "I remember very well when the first waves of B-52s came to Vietnam," he said.

"I was in Cu Chi at the time. It happened at seven P.M. We were meeting in an underground room. Everything was shaking around us." Yet nothing that occurred during the American war had the harrowing quality of the guillotinings and shootings and prison camps of Diem's Denunciation of Communists campaign. Those were the worst years, Mr. Linh said, "a ferocious time."

Of the 8,000 to 10,000 ordered to stay in the South in 1954, only about 2,000 to 2,500 survived. "I was nearly arrested many times," Mr. Linh said. "Had I been arrested, I would not be talking to you now." ("Our lives were counted in days and hours," one of Mr. Linh's fellow winter cadres remembered.) It was a relief, Mr. Linh said, when guerrilla warfare resumed at the end of the 1950s and they could shoot back.

In the meantime Ho Chi Minh and the other Communist leaders had let loose a horror of their own in the North in the mid-1950s—a Chinese-style land reform campaign orchestrated by Truong Chinh, then general secretary and chief ideologue of the Party. Thousands of real and purported landlords were tried before kangaroo courts and shot, and their families left to starve.

Somehow Nguyen Van Linh emerged in 1975 from prisons and manhunts and wars with an open mind, a sense of humor, and an enterprising spirit—and they quickly got him into trouble. His stature was so high with Le Duan, now general secretary, and other members of the old guard in Hanoi like Pham Van Dong that in 1978 he was appointed chairman of the government body that was to oversee the absorption of the South, the so-called Socialist Transformation Commission for South Vietnam. He surprised and angered his mentors by advocating a mixed economy in which "patriotic capitalists," that is, those who had stayed and were willing to cooperate with the new rulers, would be allowed to keep their factories and businesses. He also argued against the collectivization of agriculture. "The correct way would have been to help the peasants in the South to cultivate their own land as farmers do in the United States," Mr. Linh said. Southern farmers would then have had "all the incentives to increase production and be efficient."

He was denounced for "right-wing" thinking and his proposals rejected. Le Duan and the old guard went ahead with their plan to impose on the South the same centralized economy that prevailed in the North by seizing all privately owned factories and businesses and forcing Southern farmers into state cooperatives. A dour authoritarianism prevailed. Mr. Linh was appalled. "Socialism does not equal austerity and cannot be identified with a soldier's camp where there is a uniform and the same meals for everyone," he said.

Mr. Linh had not abandoned the concern for social justice first aroused in him by *Les Misérables*. "As a Communist I should always think of the interests of working people," he said. Rather, he had decided that orthodox socialism did not serve those interests because it was a foolish dream that would bankrupt the country. The touchstone of his thinking was, ironically, the lesson he had learned fighting the United States in the South: nothing worked unless it was firmly grounded in reality.

"The war against the Americans was not a war between equals; the U.S. Army was stronger than we were and had more weapons," Mr. Linh said. The Vietnamese would have lost had they simply traded blows. They had to devise a means within their grasp of wearing down the strength of their American opponent. "My comrades and I could not afford to be subjective in our conclusions. Had we been subjective, we would immediately have been crushed by reality," Mr. Linh said. "So I continued to think according to that pattern when I shifted to peaceful restructuring."

By 1982, when Mr. Linh's persistence in his odd-man-out stance had exhausted the patience of Le Duan and other senior Party figures and he was ejected from the inner circle by being kicked out of the Politburo, he was ready to leave Hanoi and the Politburo anyway. He was offered a return to a post he had previously held, Party secretary for Ho Chi Minh City, as a way of easing him into retirement. Mr. Linh did not see the job as a tombstone: "Ho Chi Minh City was a very useful testing ground for my ideas." There were men and women in Saigon with whom he had shared the experience of the American war, who had also learned from it to think in the creative, unorthodox way he did, and who would support him. "That's why I left the Politburo with a light heart," he said.

From Saigon Mr. Linh began waging economic guerrilla warfare against Hanoi. He encouraged state factory managers in the Ho Chi Minh City area to act on their own initiative; he authorized private business ventures as well. "Inspection delegations" were sent down from Hanoi to record Mr. Linh's misdeeds. The confrontation became extremely tense.

He got away with his defiance because the man and the moment were unique. In an age of monumental slaughters to settle scores, the Vietnamese Communists behaved with comparative restraint toward their defeated opponents after the victory in 1975. The much-feared "bloodbath" did not occur. Instead, nearly 100,000 persons, almost all of them former Saigon army officers and government officials, were imprisoned for years (the number of years depended on the individual's rank and record) in "reeducation camps." Conditions were grim, but the reeducation camps were not like Nazi death camps or the Japanese prison camps of World War II in which half of the inmates perished. Ninety-four thousand of the reeducation camp prisoners survived and were released.

The explanation for the restraint was complicated. The leadership feared a repetition of the bloody excesses of the land reform campaign of the 1950s. The thirty years of war since 1945 had pitted neighbor against neighbor and family member against family member, and trials and executions would only have added to the bitterness. There also seems to be an element of forbearance and proportion in Vietnamese culture, suppressed during the years of war, that reemerged in its aftermath. (The one group to which the Vietnamese Communists did exhibit great cruelty during the postwar years was the Chinese minority in Vietnam. Fearing that the Chinese might become a fifth column for Beijing, the Vietnamese authorities expelled many of them, and, as "boat people," thousands perished on the sea.)

For all his tyrannical dogmatism, Le Duan never attempted to acquire the personal power of Mao Tse-tung and purge those who opposed him in a Vietnamese version of China's Cultural Revolution. As a "veteran of the Party" with an impeccable revolutionary and war record, Mr. Linh had a standing in the postwar politics of Vietnam that could not be denied. He could be fired as Party secretary for Ho Chi Minh City, just as he had been thrown out of the Politburo, but he could not be arrested and imprisoned or executed.

The relentless deterioration in Vietnam's economic and social conditions created enough doubt in Hanoi to keep him from being fired. Mr. Linh reinforced the doubt by inviting members of the old guard like Pham Van Dong to Ho Chi Minh City to look at factories and enterprises there and see that his way worked. By 1986, when Le Duan died, the reform movement was in the ascendancy. In yet another irony, Truong Chinh, the fanatic of the 1950s who had been disgraced by the land reform campaign and not permitted to hold an executive office until he became interim general secretary on Le Duan's death, promoted Mr. Linh's candidacy for the post at the Sixth Party Congress that year. In a speech to the congress he attacked the postwar attempt to create an orthodox Marxist state as a colossal error. He too had been invited to Ho Chi Minh City by Mr. Linh to see a different way. "Nothing is stronger than reality," Mr. Linh said.

Mr. Linh has often been called the Vietnamese Gorbachev, and up to a point there is some aptness in the comparison. He is a man of the system without being a captive of the system. The difference was that Mr. Linh seemed to have a firmer grasp of the end result he wanted and to be prepared to risk drastic economic change to achieve it. "Socialism is prosperity," he said. And while not abandoning his earlier principles, he was willing to compromise on them. The free enterprise element of the mixed economy he envisioned meant social inequities; it also meant jobs Vietnamese so desperately needed: "We have to accept a certain level of exploitation."

The predicament was how to achieve the end result. It was obvious that until Vietnam could obtain enough foreign business investment and financing from the international lending institutions to build the infrastructure necessary for a modern economy, the country was going to remain poor. The process could not begin to occur on a major scale until the American embargo was lifted, and then the task of bringing it to fruition would take years. Vietnam came to terms with China in the fall of 1991 and the two countries resumed peaceable relations, but the United States continued its boycott. In the meantime the radical measures adopted by Mr. Linh and his adherents could improve the country's lot but not genuinely stabilize a fragile economy. The inflation they held in check during 1989 began to rise again during 1990 and was exceeding 100 percent a year by the end of 1991.

Time had also run out on Mr. Linh in his mid-seventies. The vitality of this trim man, with his steel gray hair combed straight, his alert eyes under the salt-and-pepper brows, was deceptive. He had an episode of colon cancer in 1988 and underwent surgery in Russia. There had been no recurrence, but his health was precarious. He was not the boss in Vietnam; rather, the first among equals. The element of restraint that protected him when he was a dissident worked against him after he became general secretary.

Decision making in Vietnam is by consensus. To act, the general secretary has to convince the other twelve members of the Politburo to go along with him. The naysayers can always slow him down by failing to agree. When I saw him, Mr. Linh was attempting to place protégés, men in their fifties and sixties whom he trusted to carry on his ideas, in positions of authority. Because of his age and health he was determined to retire at the Seventh Party Congress in 1991, when he would be seventy-six. "You cannot resist nature. I shall be a wrongdoer if I remain at my post," he said. The other old men also had their protégés and sometimes blocked his appointments. Yet he was convinced he had made a start, and events seemed to bear him out. When the Seventh Party Congress came, he did retire and was succeeded as general secretary by a Northerner he had converted to his thinking, Do Muoi, and he maneuvered into the prime ministership his friend and subordinate in the jungle, Vo Van Kiet.

His conviction that he had set his country on a course from which there was no full turning back and the simplicity of his life gave one the impression of a man who is at peace with himself. Mr. Linh's home in Saigon is an unpretentious house where he and his wife encourage the presence of their grandchildren. Does he still play Ping-Pong, as I had heard he liked to do? "No more Ping-Pong . . . well, perhaps from time to time. I do every day a kind of gymnastics appropriate for old people," he explained. He laughed as he mimicked himself at these exercises, breathing rhythmically and rotating his hands through the air. The exercises were called *tai chi.* Mr. Linh performed them for a half hour after he woke at five A.M., the same time he had gotten up every day in the jungle.

The main Communist headquarters where Mr. Linh had served as deputy during the war was called the Central Office for South Vietnam. The U.S. military, with its love of acronyms, shortened this to COSVN, and "COSVN" became synonymous with "mystery" because the American generals were constantly trying to find it and never succeeding. Richard Nixon announced on national television that he was going to destroy it during his sweep into Cambodia in 1970; he did not find COSVN either. I had heard that the final location of the headquarters was being preserved in the jungle. Could Susan and I go there? I asked Mr. Linh. "Of course you can," he said. Then he left as he had come, in the back of the off-white Lada, with just one security guard up front, to spend the rest of that Sunday with his family.

Many of the big trees had been cut to let the light come down. It was no longer necessary to hide the thatched huts from the cameras of the American spy satellites and the eyes of the spotter plane pilots. Someone had planted flowers along the path leading from the nearby post of the Frontier Guards who watched over this sylvan place and its memories.

Our escort, Huynh Van Ngoc, remembered that when he had first been assigned to COSVN in 1962 this region out on the Cambodian border had been so wild that tigers and elephants were nearly as common as people. It was a memory I shared with him because I had come out here then on helicopter assaults as a correspondent with the ARVN troops and their American advisors, who were searching for Mr. Ngoc and his companions. Once in a while we had discovered traces—a rain forest arms workshop making road mines to blow up military convoys or shotguns to distribute to hamlet guerrillas; a small camp abandoned as we approached, the volleyball net still up, food still in the cooking pots. Usually we had found only the dense maze of the hardwood underbrush under the high teak and mahogany trees whose canopy of branches darkened the forest at midday. The Vietnamese on Mr. Ngoc's side had appropriately called the region War Zone R, for *rung*, meaning "forest."

The tigers and the elephants were gone, a casualty not of the war but of Vietnam's alarming population growth. The rain forest was receding rapidly before the saws and axes of settlers seeking new farmland and loggers feeding the Saigon sawmills and the export trade to Japan. In the old days people became scarce and the forest commenced soon after the road passed Tay Ninh, the provincial capital northwest of Saigon where the Cao Dai religious sect had built its cathedral, a pastel astonishment that would have startled Walt Disney, painted anew each year to preserve its wonder, in a two-hundred-acre park. The round mass of Black Virgin Mountain (Nui Ba Den) still rose with dramatic suddenness out of the plain beyond the town, but the stripping away of the mystery of its rain forest mantle, begun by the Americans with defoliants sprayed from aircraft, had been completed by people. Gray boulders formerly hidden by trees bulged out amidst scrub brush. The lower slopes were busy with banana groves and plantings of manioc; higher up the farmers had cleared pastures for their cattle and goats.

Where in the past one was rarely out of the sight of trees, one was now seldom out of the sight of people as the hamlets marched along the road almost to the border post at Xa Mat. Many of the settlers' houses were also a rarity for rural Vietnam. The walls were of wide, rough-sawn planks rather than wicker because the wood that was so valuable in Saigon was cheap and plentiful out here. In the distance, beyond the new rice fields, an occasional grove of tall trees bore witness to what once had been.

The officials at the postwar district center created to administer the area, now called Tan Bien—literally, "New Border"—were getting rich on their rake-off from the smuggling from Cambodia and the logging operations. They had bought themselves a brand-new Toyota van in which to run around. They were being paid so handsomely, in fact, that no one bothered to hide what was going on. Groups of big cab-over-engine trucks with Cambodian lettering on the doors frequently rolled past, headed east into the interior of Vietnam. Neatly roped tarpaulins covered the loads in the back, but the consumer plenty of Saigon and the displays of VCRs and TVs and the choices of beer—Carlsberg or Sapporo for those bored with Heineken—in the marketplaces of the towns we had passed through explained what was under the canvas.

An expanse of young rubber trees near Xa Mat hid another kind of tale—the story of the different fear that had come to the border regions after the American war. The trees covered the site where an entire hamlet of Vietnamese had been massacred by the Khmer Rouge troops of Pol Pot. The Vietnamese are bitter at the failure of most of the world to understand why they invaded Cambodia to overthrow him and attribute it to the combined power of China, Pol Pot's patron, and the United States, China's tacit ally in Cambodian events, to influence international opinion.

They argue that they had no choice, and the facts lend substance to their argument. Most students of Southeast Asian affairs agree that the attacks, which began intermittently right after the fall of Saigon in 1975 and became serious by 1977, were initiated by the Khmer Rouge (the term derives from a French one meaning "Red Khmers," i.e., Cambodian Communists), and were pressed relentlessly despite Vietnamese attempts at conciliation. The majority of the towns and villages along the border had to be evacuated because of raids and constant shelling by the Pol Potists with mortars and artillery pieces supplied by China. (China also sent hundreds of military advisors to Cambodia to guide Pol Pot's army.)

Massacres such as the one at Xa Mat were particularly hideous because the Khmer Rouge, which caused the deaths of 700,000 to 1,000,000 of their own people in a four-year reign of terror, specialized in beheadings and atrocities like the eviscerating of pregnant women. By December 1978, the Vietnamese had suffered approximately 30,000 troops killed in two years of border fighting, an equivalent number of civilians dead, tens of thousands of wounded, the destruction of thousands of homes and public build-ings, and the wholesale abandonment of border farmlands. At the end of that month the Vietnamese Army invaded Cambodia and within two weeks chased Pol Pot and the remnants of his forces over to the Thai frontier. The Cambodian people, fearful and starving, momentarily forgot the centuries of enmity and welcomed the Vietnamese as their deliverers. The Vietnamese installed a client regime in Phnom Penh headed by Heng Samrin, Hun Sen, and other leaders of the anti–Pol Pot faction of the Cambodian Communist Party.

The fighting, however, did not stop. At the urging of Washing-ton and Beijing, Thailand protected Pol Pot and his followers in border sanctuaries while China and the United States connived at rebuilding the Khmer Rouge into a potent guerrilla force. By the time Vietnam withdrew the last of its army almost ten years later at the end of September 1989, leaving behind military advisors and a small backup force to sustain the Phnom Penh regime, the Vietnamese had lost another 25,300 soldiers dead and 55,000 seriously wounded. In all, nearly as many Vietnamese soldiers died in the border clashes and subsequently in Cambodia itself as Americans did in the whole of the Vietnam War. The Vietnamese wondered rhetorically what the United States would have done if a government like Pol Pot's had come to power in Canada and launched assaults on Detroit and other cities along the American-Canadian border.

At Xa Mat the recollection of Pol Pot was vivid. The rubber

trees were planted on the site of the hamlet because no one would live there anymore out of memory of the horror. Farther down the road was another souvenir—a large earth wall running parallel to the frontier that had been erected as a fortification. A few hundred yards past it were the Vietnamese and Cambodian customs posts, which face each other across the border itself. Three more smuggling trucks were waiting at the Vietnamese post to pay their bribes.

A secondary dirt road turned off the main one at Xa Mat and once again ran north along the border through forest. Loggers were busy felling big trees and loading them onto trucks like the one we had seen at the Ho Chi Minh City Arts and Literature Association, but there were no houses anymore. Mr. Ngoc said that the usual dangers of logging were compounded out here near the border by Chinese antipersonnel mines that Pol Pot's troops had planted among the trees. The mines retained their sensitivity because they were made of plastic that did not deteriorate and for the same reason were difficult to detect until a logger stepped on one.

About ten miles into the forest the road encountered a stream. The Toyota van carrying the district staff was in the lead. It forded the stream fully loaded. We had to evacuate the lower-slung Russian Volga sedan we had rented in Saigon so that the driver could get it across. A little way beyond was a dirt clearing with a flagpole and three thatched buildings—the post of the Frontier Guards who patrol this section of the border and still protect from unwelcome eyes that which the American military sought and never found. The flagpole was bare. The Vietnamese national emblem, a gold star on a red field that first flew as the flag of Ho's Viet Minh in 1945, had just been given a washing and was hanging to dry with other laundry on a line next to the plank-sided building that served as the post headquarters and home for the lieutenant in command and his deputy.

Lacking cold-storage facilities, the Vietnamese Army kept its chickens fresh—clucking in cages on one side of the room. A "boom box" cassette player was hooked up to a car battery beside a bunk in a corner. A single fluorescent light, powered by the post's small portable generator, hung over a plank table and benches. Mr. Ngoc gave the lieutenant a stack of paperback books he had brought out from Saigon to help the soldiers pass the time. "These men know what a hard life is," he said.

In the morning on the way out from Saigon Mr. Ngoc had stopped the car in the marketplace at Go Dau Ha, where the road forks for Tay Ninh, and bought a cluster of incense sticks. I learned why as soon as we walked past the post and down the path into the trees beyond to one of the open-sided huts in the old headquarters. A photograph of a gray-haired man hung from a roof beam at one end of the hut. In front of the photograph was a traditional Vietnamese altar, homemade of split bamboo, with a small sand-filled urn on it in which to place burning incense sticks.

Mr. Ngoc stood before the altar, lit the cluster of sticks, slowly lifted them toward the photograph with the smoke of the incense rising as he bowed his head, then gave each of us a burning stick to place in the sand of the urn. The photograph was a picture of the hut's occupant during the war, Pham Hung, born in the Mekong Delta in 1912; joined Ho Chi Minh's Revolutionary Youth League as a lycée student radical in the 1920s; condemned to the guillotine in 1931, a sentence commuted to penal servitude for life on Poulo Condore, where he was another of Nguyen Van Linh's prisonmates but there for longer, fourteen years; led the war in the South as head of COSVN and delegate of the Politburo from 1967 until the victory in 1975; appointed prime minister of Vietnam in 1987 as a supporter of reform; died in Saigon of a heart attack in 1988 after a meeting at which he urged a faster pace of change; and at this shrine in the forest entered the centuries-old pantheon of Vietnam's warrior mandarins whose spirits are worshipped with incense and homage.

Pham Hung's hut is one of half a dozen that remain of a community in which five to six hundred people once lived and worked under the protection of the trees. Immense care was taken so that nothing could be seen from overhead. Gaps in the natural camouflage of the forest canopy were filled by tying the branches of trees together or suspending trellises of bamboo and covering them with brush and freshly cut boughs. Similar precautions applied to sound and light. The gasoline generators that provided power for the radios and the lighting were placed in pits to muffle the noise. Curtains of black plastic or nylon were hung over the sides of the huts at night to block the light. The security battalion kept troops dispersed in listening posts for several miles in every direction to prevent surprise.

The huts of the leaders like Pham Hung were pavilions about fifteen feet wide and thirty feet long, with plenty of overhang in the roofs to deflect the rain and hard-tamped earth floors built up about a foot and a half above the surrounding ground to keep them dry. The main upright posts, the cross beams, and the roof joists were stripped clean of bark and joined together by pegs; no nails had been used. The roofs were thatched with a long leaf called the "loyal leaf," because legend says one of the emperors used it for thatch during his campaigns. Imperial lineage was not the reason this particular leaf was employed as roofing material at COSVN. It was used because it had a natural fire-retardant quality in the event of a napalm strike or an accident. One of the men from the district staff demonstrated by tearing off a piece and trying to set it on fire with his cigarette lighter. The leaf would not stay lit.

The sides of the huts were left open for maximum ventilation and comfort in the daytime. Mr. Ngoc remembered that at this last location there had always been some movement of air, even in the hottest season in March and April before the monsoon, because the forest had been a double canopy—a cover of tall trees with a fairly light growth of pole trees and brush underneath. He recalled that at earlier locations in denser triple-canopy rain forest the heat and stillness would become almost unbearable at the height of the day. After dark everyone would walk out to the nearest clearing and lie there to breathe fresh air.

In the early sixties, Mr. Ngoc said, the headquarters had always been located in this region of northwestern Tay Ninh Province, moving occasionally but not with great frequency. Everything changed after full-scale military intervention by the United States in 1965. A hide-and-seek contest with lethal consequences for the loser began as the U.S. command used every possible means of intelligence—intercepting and decoding radio traffic and locating transmitters, interrogating prisoners and defectors, analyzing captured documents, aerial and satellite photography, long-range patrols by Special Forces teams—to try to find COSVN.

Air raids, which were launched nonstop against all suspected Communist base areas, were the greatest fear of the Vietnamese, particularly B-52 strikes, for which there was no warning because the big bombers usually dropped from about 30,000 feet. Slit trenches for instant protection were dug throughout the headquarters area, and each section had underground air raid bunkers for all of its personnel. Senior leaders like Pham Hung and Linh had a bunker right under their huts so that they could seek shelter immediately if bombs began to fall while they were asleep, and another bunker nearby to which they could dash during daytime raids. The bunkers had two entrance-exits in case a hit collapsed one of the openings. An entrance to Pham Hung's outside bunker was still visible amidst some foliage about twenty yards from his hut, the opening framed in logs reinforced with cement.

Nevertheless, despite frequent moves and every other precaution by the Vietnamese, the relentless bombing won the Americans a round in the contest, although they would not learn of it until later. In 1967 Lt. Gen. Nguyen Chi Thanh, Pham Hung's predecessor as head of COSVN, was killed in a B-52 strike while the headquarters was situated only a few miles from the final location we were visiting. After that, Mr. Ngoc said, "We hid in the forests of Cambodia." The headquarters continued to shift constantly, every few months, to nullify any patterns American intelligence officers might be able to establish, but crossing the border did not bring immunity. The search went on and the bombs followed.

Mr. Ngoc remembered that the worst period came after the nationwide Communist offensive at the end of January 1968, during Tet, the Lunar New Year holiday, caught Gen. William Westmoreland by surprise. The hunt for COSVN was intensified. In 1969 Prince Norodom Sihanouk, then ruler of Cambodia, also turned against the Vietnamese and tacitly consented to wholesale

B-52 bombing in his country. Nixon ordered a series of secret raids. No other ranking figure at COSVN was killed because the headquarters was never discovered with precision, but there were close calls.

Near the end of 1972, shortly before the signing of the Paris Agreement that brought about the withdrawal of U.S. military forces, a decision was made to move back into Vietnam and set up the headquarters at this last position. The risk seemed acceptable because the Vietnamese no longer had to worry about B-52 strikes, although they still had to take precautions against raids by fighter-bombers of the Saigon government's air arm. They were shrewd enough to select an area that had already been bombed thoroughly. Pham Hung converted a crater right behind his hut, which filled with water during the rainy season, into a fish pond. (The crater is still there, full of milky water, but the fish are gone.) Despite the plentitude of streams in the area, drinking and cooking water was a problem because everyone was afraid that the defoliant chemicals had poisoned the surface supplies. The Vietnamese eased their worries by digging wells.

The hut of Nguyen Van Linh, a couple of hundred yards away down a footpath through the trees, also had a bomb crater beside it. The hut's postwar furnishings were a table and benches, and we all sat down and ate a picnic lunch in this parklike place. The photograph of Mr. Linh hanging from a roof beam above the table showed him as he appeared, in the words of Mr. Ngoc, *"dans le maquis,"* the World War II French term for a resistance zone that the older French-speaking generation of Vietnamese revolutionaries use to refer to their time in the jungle. Mr. Linh was wearing the loose-fitting, pajamalike work garb of a Vietnamese peasant and sitting on the hammock in which he slept. In his memory an identical hammock had been slung between two posts of the hut.

The days at the headquarters had gone quickly, Mr. Ngoc said, because of the routine. Each section—intelligence, communications, operations—had its work to do. A reporter for the Viet Minh press agency in the South during the French war, Mr. Ngoc was an information specialist at COSVN during the American one. At the morning briefing he would summarize and interpret the events of the previous day within Vietnam and internationally for Pham Hung, Mr. Linh, and the rest of the leadership. He typed his briefing reports on a Remington portable he had bought in 1944 while a student at the French school of commerce in Saigon and carried back down the Ho Chi Minh Trail when he returned to the South in 1962.

An elaborate skein of field telephone lines that by 1972 stretched for hundreds of miles had sufficed for much of the communication with subsidiary headquarters units. The phones were reasonably secure because they could not be intercepted like radios and the lines were patrolled to detect tapping. For longer distances the message would be encoded and then transmitted by radio operators using the old-fashioned technique of a telegraph key that beeped out dots and dashes in the Morse system. More sophisticated teletype and telex machines were not employed, Mr. Ngoc said, because the lower units would have had to possess the same equipment to receive and answer. "With Morse we could all talk to each other."

Nighttime entertainment improved together with the long-distance telephones at this last headquarters base. A number of black-and-white television sets were captured in the spring of 1972, when the North Vietnamese Army overran the district headquarters of Loc Ninh in neighboring Binh Long Province. Some of the trophy TVs were presented to COSVN. At six P.M., when the workday was over, the staff would raise the aerials and gather round to watch programs broadcast on the television network the United States had provided the Saigon regime. Favorite fare was performances by Kim Cuong, a famous Saigonese actress who turned out after the war to be a secret adherent of Ho Chi Minh.

In early April 1975, Pham Hung transferred to another headquarters near Loc Ninh to coordinate the final campaign with Gen. Van Tien Dung, who had come down from Hanoi to command it. Le Duc Tho, who had faced Henry Kissinger across the negotiating table in Paris, also arrived from the North. Just before the culminating assault on Saigon they shifted to a last secret headquarters near Ben Cat, only twenty-five miles north of the city. Mr. Linh stayed behind at COSVN to relay messages and keep track of things. On the morning of May 1, the day after Saigon fell, everyone at COSVN marched out to the road, loaded their gear onto trucks, and, in a convoy led by Mr. Linh, headed for the city denied them so long.

They drove all day because the roads were crowded with troop columns, artillery, tanks, and armored personnel carriers. At Tan Son Nhut, which they reached at five P.M., there was so much confusion that they pushed on to the Saigon regime's police academy at Thu Duc in the hope of finding a place to set up camp and sleep. But disorder and overcrowding drove them on again, this time to the Saigon University faculty housing village on the Bien Hoa Highway. "The professors had run away," Mr. Ngoc said. They settled in for the night. Mr. Ngoc had brought his Remington portable along. He still types on it at the Party secretariat in Ho Chi Minh City.

Ben Suc and its people had taken nearly the worst a superpower could give. In January 1967, the village was one of the focal points of a U.S. Army scorched-earth operation aimed at destroying a Communist guerrilla base known as the Iron Triangle in the rubber plantation country north of Saigon. Almost all the inhabitants were rounded up and forcibly removed in helicopters, trucks, and river landing craft, their houses and family graves bulldozed behind them. Those who hid and stayed with the guerrillas were strafed by day and hunted at night by special "Night Hawk" helicopter teams that had searchlights to catch the unwary and trap them in the glare for the machine gunners aboard. The Americans made war on the land too, blasting it with bombs and shells, searing it with napalm and white phosphorous munitions, stripping it of trees and vegetation by spraying it with defoliants.

Phan Van Chinh remembered the day the American soldiers came. He was the Party secretary for the village then as well as commander of the village guerrillas. He had been tipped off that the attack was going to occur, but he decided to stay and try to organize what resistance he could from a hiding place in a bamboo grove near the council house where I met him when I went to the village to find out what had become of Ben Suc. A 1967 account by Jonathan Schell of its devastation, published in *The New Yorker*, had made the name notorious during the war, a synonym for the wastelands created in South Vietnam by the "search and destroy" strategy of General Westmoreland.

Ben Suc was at the northwest corner of the Iron Triangle, the lines of which delineated, in a fashion more symbolic than precise, the heartland of two renowned Communist districts above Saigon—Cu Chi and Ben Cat. The origins of Communist strength in the region went back to colonial conditions on the French rubber plantations. When they arrived at a plantation, Vietnamese workers were deprived of their names and assigned numbers for identification. The death rate from disease and maltreatment ran to about 25 percent. The area became a political stronghold of Communist labor organizing in the 1930s, and after 1945 a military stronghold too when the rubber workers and the farmers in the villages around the plantations took up the cause of Ho Chi Minh with vehemence during the first war for independence from France.

Because of its proximity to Saigon, the base was regarded as a major menace. The initial attempt to wipe it out during the American war occurred in the early 1960s. The population was herded into "strategic hamlets," fortified and guarded enclosures surrounded by barbed wire. In an irrepressible Panglossianism that sometimes bordered on the obscene, the U.S. mission in Saigon had dubbed the first of these early forced relocations "Operation Sunrise." The Viet Cong guerrillas soon grew strong enough to overrun the enclosures and turn the peasants loose to rebuild their original homes.

The Saigon forces then resorted to bombing and shelling to try to drive out the peasantry, but that tactic also failed. The farmers, Mr. Chinh explained, were reluctant to abandon rice fields and fruit orchards that produced abundantly on land rich from the silt of the Saigon River for the poverty of refugee camps, and, despite the greater ferocity of this second war, the peasants were as stalwart as ever in their support of the Communist cause. After the Johnson administration intervened in full force in 1965, the U.S. Army generals decided that mass evacuation and razing were the solution to the problem.

The council house where I met him did not exist on that morning in January 1967 when the helicopters arrived, Mr. Chinh said. There was a soccer field there, and two of the helicopters used it as a landing zone. Other helicopters set down along a road leading to a ferry point at a loop in the Saigon River that formed the lower boundary of the village.

Gray now and in his mid-sixties, Mr. Chinh had no sight in his left eye and his left leg was useless, frozen at the knee—injuries from an American artillery shell that burst near him in a later year of the war. He had also lost all of the teeth on the left side of his mouth, and he had to wear glasses with a thick lens to see with the eye that remained. He still had a commanding voice, and he spoke with animation as he told the story, pointing down emphatically when he described how the first helicopter landed right where the council house was subsequently built.

Approximately 10,000 people were evacuated from Ben Suc. The population of the village normally ran to about 5,600 in those days, Mr. Chinh said, but it had nearly been doubled by the families who had been bombed out of neighboring villages and taken shelter with friends and relatives. The Americans brought with them their Vietnamese allies, the soldiers of the Saigon government's army. The U.S. troops created cordons around each of the hamlets within the village and sent the ARVN soldiers inside to do the rounding up.

Many of the people were herded with whatever belongings they could carry onto big cargo helicopters that arrived after the smaller assault helicopters had brought in American infantrymen to secure the area. Others were marched down to the ferry point at the river and loaded onto landing craft that pulled up there. Those who tried to run away were shot. U.S. Army bulldozers demolished about 950 houses, leveling the village. The bulldozer blades even broke the bricks, Mr. Chinh said. Only 340 of the original inhabitants managed to hide and stay behind, and from that day forward, like the guerrillas, they had to live virtually underground in dugouts and tunnels.

By April 30, 1975, it was hard to find a building of any description still standing in the entire area. The official U.S. Army maps illustrate what occurred. A 1967-edition map shows the main dirt road connecting the village to the outside world as a well-surfaced one usable in the rainy season. On the 1972-edition map a thin broken line indicates that the road had been reduced to an oxcart track.

It took ten years to rebuild the village and reclaim the land. About fifty people were killed or wounded by unexploded bombs, mines, and grenades hidden in the brush and the earth that detonated when accidentally hit by an implement during land clearing and cultivation. An American 40mm grenade shell from a weapon called the M-79 was a particular menace because the fuse was armed as the shell spun out of the barrel and a slight disturbance was all that was necessary to set off a dud lying on the ground.

Reconstruction started right after the Communist victory in 1975, Nguyen Thanh Liem, the current Party secretary for the village, said. A slim, bold-spoken man in his early thirties, Mr. Liem had been taken from Ben Suc as a ten-year-old child and spent his youth in the resettlement area farther south and closer to Saigon, where the families had been forced to live. They had been eager to return because the land had been poor there and no one had been able to earn a living. They had subsisted on what they could grow and on handouts for refugees.

Mr. Liem, who had succeeded Mr. Chinh as Party secretary only the year before, had not been expecting American visitors to his village. I had decided to make a trip to Ben Suc one of our first excursions out of Saigon. During the early 1960s I had often been in the Cu Chi and Ben Cat districts on operations with the ARVN troops and their American advisors and once in Ben Suc itself on a helicopter assault long before it was razed. The experience had invariably been harrowing.

The population had been strikingly militant. In most Communist-dominated areas, the peasant children would smile at the odd-looking Americans; in Cu Chi and Ben Cat the stares of the children were as hostile as those of the adults. During a helicopter landing at an outpost in the area, it was the rule rather than the exception to take a hit in the machine or hear a bullet crack past the open door. Traveling in road convoys was especially unnerving because one never knew when the convoy was going to be ambushed or a vehicle blown up by a mine. I wanted to return to the most notoriously punished village in this place that had so unbendingly opposed us, hear from these people what they had endured for their commitment, and see how they had fared in the years of peace.

Thang and Tien, who were boys in the North when Ben Suc was leveled, had no idea where it was, but I knew the approximate location and I had the wartime U.S. Army maps I had brought to Vietnam to use in guiding the driver. We set off northwest from Saigon on a Saturday morning in the rented Volga, a sturdy vehicle built like a 1960s Chevrolet.

When questions at the marketplace and the council house determined that we had found the right village (the official name is Thanh Tuyen, but the locals still call the village by its original name of Ben Suc), someone sent for Mr. Liem. He then dispatched the Volga, with a villager to give the driver directions, for Mr. Chinh and two other older veterans of the Ben Suc guerrillas. Because it was a Saturday, Mr. Liem had been drinking rice wine at a wedding party and his face was a bit flushed. Once everyone was assembled, several young women appeared with trays of refreshing iced washcloths and green coconuts with straws to drink the milk.

As with other communities where most of the population had sided with the Communists during the war and suffered severely for it, the central government helped to finance the reconstruction of Ben Suc. The council house had been the first substantial structure to be built—in 1978. A clinic and a one-story red brick schoolhouse with enough classroom capacity to take the village children through the twelfth grade ("But not as comfortable as the old school," Mr. Liem remarked) had followed in the 1980s.

The council house consisted of two small wings for village offices and a larger room in the center where we sat. This larger room had wooden benches and a podium in front for meetings of the People's Committee, the term for the village government, and the village branch of the Vietnamese Communist Party. On the wall behind the podium were hand-painted portraits of Karl Marx, Lenin, and Ho Chi Minh. Marx wore a red bow tie and a beard that, in the painting, looked like the wide starched collar of a seventeenth-century English Puritan gentleman.

There were still bomb craters all over the place, each an arduous task to fill in, and the villagers were convinced that the defoliants, usually referred to as Agent Orange after the most common one, had permanently weakened the soil. All the older people in the room nodded assent when Mr. Liem said that in prewar years no fertilizer had been necessary for rice growing. The silt from the Saigon River had sufficed. Now fertilizer was necessary, and fruit trees were said to bear less than before. "I'm a fruit farmer," Mr. Liem said, flashing the palms of his hands to show the calluses and demonstrate that his newly gained stature had not turned him into a bureaucrat.

Susan and I asked to see the new school and walked down to it from the council house. In front of the schoolyard was a bomb crater the villagers had nearly finished filling, originally one of a string of two to three hundred craters from a B-52 strike that had been laid right through Ben Suc. Mr. Liem looked at the shallow dip that still remained in the ground and said of the crater-elimination task, "Little by little." Behind the vegetable garden of a nearby house was a yet-unfilled crater, about twenty-five feet across and fifteen deep. It was not noticeable from a distance because the homeowner had planted bamboo inside to make some use of the hole, and the bamboo had grown tall enough to disguise it. The giveaway was a fence around the edge to keep livestock from falling in and breaking a leg.

I was puzzled by the area in front of the new infirmary—humpy ground growing wild. The brush-covered humps were what was left of a family graveyard that had been partially leveled by the U.S. Army bulldozers. Mr. Liem said the American soldiers had discovered some Viet Cong tunnels nearby and apparently bulldozed the graves to block the entrances. The family concerned refused to either restore the graves or move the remains elsewhere, and so the ground was untouchable.

By now it was late afternoon. A pair of carts drawn by teams of oxen was heading down the road out of the village toward the rubber plantation behind Ben Suc. In this part of the country the clack, clack, clack of the wooden cart wheels was a sound I had never associated with dwindling daylight. Guerrilla activity had tended to increase in direct proportion to the approach of dusk, and a setting sun meant rising bursts of automatic weapons fire and the crash of incoming mortar shells.

In addition to rebuilding their own village, the people of Ben Suc had also played the major role in restoring the plantation. During the war rubber plantations were favored places for the Viet Cong to hide and fight. The foliage gave concealment, and the arrangement of the trees in rows provided deadly lanes for fields of fire. As a result, rubber plantations, the principal agricultural resource of the South after rice farming, were systematically eradicated under "Operation Ranch Hand," the U.S. Air Force's code name for the defoliation. The old Guibert Plantation behind Ben Suc was no exception. Virtually all of its trees had been poisoned and had withered away. The place was now a Vietnamese government enterprise founded with Soviet economic assistance. The villagers of Ben Suc had, however, planted most of its five thousand new trees in return for wages and the promise of a share in the profits when the trees produced marketable latex in another few years.

Mr. Liem asked if we wanted to take a ride into the plantation to see the last grove of original trees. As he climbed into the front seat of the car, he put on a denim cap in the baseball style currently favored by American farmers as working headgear. The old rubber trees in the grove looked like the survivors they were, gnarled and misshapen from the combined effects of age, the defoliants, and limbs slashed off by flying shrapnel. There were about fifty acres left in this grove of the hundreds that once had been. Mr. Liem pointed to tall grass growing in the open space between the trees and the plantation road. We encountered it all over the South in areas that had been defoliated. The Vietnamese called it "American grass." They claimed, without any precise evidence, that the planes had spray-planted it after defoliating the original vegetation because during the dry season it could easily be set afire with napalm and white phosphorous bombs. Whatever its origin, the grass, which resembled timothy, was not native to Vietnam and had not existed there before the war. With their limited grazing needs, the Vietnamese farmers had little use for it and regarded it as an exasperating weed.

Two wild ducks flew overhead in the dusk, heading for night haven on the Saigon River after stealing a meal from someone's rice paddy. Even with the twisted trees and the unwanted grass, the scene was pastoral. We drove back to Saigon in the darkness along the dirt roads that had once been so terrifying in the day, the glow of the kerosene lamps in the peasant houses beckoning to us. It was as if there had never been anything but peace in this land.

The difference between Hanoi and Saigon was sitting across from me in the rooftop dining room of the Hotel Caravelle—a military security officer having an expensive lunch, a gold ballpoint pen in the breast pocket of his neatly laundered uniform. The difference was also parked in the square out in front of the hotel—a white BMW sedan in the largest 7000 series. A sticker on the rear window said it had been purchased from the Ronnie Lau Trading Company, 273 Thomson Road, Singapore: "Specialists in buying, selling and exporting secondhand Mercedes-Benz, Jaguar, and BMW cars." The license plates, green with white lettering, were the kind issued to Vietnamese civilian government agencies. A crook in Hanoi would not think of using misappropriated public funds to buy a BMW as his allegedly official car. There no one would dare to flaunt corruption so openly. The capital of the South may have been renamed Ho Chi Minh City, but long after Nguyen Van Linh, Mr. Ngoc, and their comrades had come in from the forest, the ways of the Saigon they conquered lingered to shape the society they were trying to build.

The South is Vietnam's California, and Saigon is its Los Angeles. The Vietnamese have lived in the Red River delta of the North for thousands of years. The strength there has always been tradition and the pride and self-respect engendered by long-honored ways of behavior. During a walk on one of our first nights in Hanoi, I noticed how keenly that pride was felt. A little girl approached me with her hand stretched out to beg. Her mother was sitting on the sidewalk selling cigarettes. The woman leapt up, grabbed the child by the arm, and slapped her face. The mother was probably as hungry as the little girl, but she was not going to permit her daughter to beg.

The South, in contrast, is a relatively new place for the Vietnamese. They have lived in Saigon and the Mekong delta in large numbers only since the 1700s, after they conquered the region from the Cambodians who had settled it earlier. The strength of the South has been the freewheeling spirit that arose from this newness. Much that was unseemly accompanied that spirit. As the Vietnamese say, "When you open the door to the breeze, the dirt comes in too." In Saigon the child would have been sent to beg. Yet with that spirit also came an enterprise one did not see in the North. The enterprise was being nurtured in Saigon by the infrastructure of hotels and office buildings left over from the American war and in the Mekong delta by the much-improved road system the United States had built in its vain attempt to pacify the country.

Not that nothing had changed in the unseemly side of Saigon. The city had undergone a catharsis since 1975. There were beggars and prostitutes, but not the legions of both that had existed during the American war. Many homeless slept on the sidewalks at night, but there were no teeming warrens like the slums of the peasant refugees who had fled the American bombing and shelling of the countryside. While corruption was serious, it did not approach the fundamentally corrupt nature of the old Saigon regime, where everything was for sale.

The question that most immediately determined status in postwar Saigon and in the postwar society of the South as a whole was: What did you or your family do during the war? The South, both urban and rural, was a society run by veterans or, as at Ben Suc where young Mr. Liem was the current Party secretary, those whom the veterans had chosen to succeed them. One saw the pattern right away in the people who dominated Saigon. They were winter cadres like Mr. Linh who had not gone to the North after the defeat of the French in 1954 but had stayed the full course of the struggle in the South through Diem and the Americans.

Saigon's business tycoon, Nguyen Thi Thi, or Ba Thi (Mrs. Thi), as she was called, still dressed as she had in the jungle, in the light cotton blouse and loose-fitting black pantaloons of a peasant woman. Not to be denied her eccentricity, Mrs. Thi also wore a peasant's conical straw hat as she moved about managing her multimillion-dollar companies. A native of the Mekong delta like one of her earlier patrons, Pham Hung, she had participated in the first Communist-led rebellion there against the French in 1940 when she was eighteen, and had lost her husband to Diem's guillotine in 1959. He had been arrested because he was Party secretary for the Saigon suburb of Gia Dinh. She had escaped with her two daughters and spent the American war as head of the Viet Cong Women's Federation.

There was nothing rustic about her talent for making money. She had turned a rice distribution network for Ho Chi Minh City into a conglomerate that included the Ho Chi Minh City Food Company, still the major purveyor of rice in the city but the maker as well of more than two hundred other products for domestic consumption and export—everything from manioc crackers to noodles to cashew nuts; a separate rice-processing and rice-export enterprise financed by Japanese capital; a bank; and the country's first oil refinery, Saigon Petro.

Mrs. Thi became a businesswoman by force of circumstance. When the farmers of the delta reduced planting after they were driven into cooperatives in 1978 under Le Duan's orthodox Marxism, she could no longer get enough rice to feed the city. Mr. Linh, then still in his first term as the city's Party secretary, let her start obtaining and selling rice at market value, which stimulated output because she gave the farmers she dealt with a fair return. The experiment provoked anger in Hanoi. "When you worked legally, it was irrational, but when you worked rationally, then it was illegal," Mrs. Thi said of those years. "The only way to convince people is to succeed."

One of Mrs. Thi's assistants, who did the interpreting in the second-floor conference room of her new rice-processing mill in Binh Chanh District, six miles south of Saigon, illuminated, through his lack of it, the status that gave her the freedom to succeed. He spoke colloquial American English better than the best interpreters we had encountered in the North, who said they had learned their English in Cuba during the war from left-wing Americans belonging to something called the Venceremos (We Will Conquer) Brigade. When four Japanese men in hard hats walked into the room in the middle of the interview, we discovered that Mrs. Thi's assistant spoke colloquial Japanese too. He greeted them and translated a couple of questions from Mrs. Thi before the interview resumed. Only Mrs. Thi had so far attracted significant Japanese capital—$7.5 million on a two-year loan from Satake Engineering to equip the Binh Chanh facility—because her position and track record made investing with her safe. She was paying off the loan with exports of Mekong delta rice processed at the mill.

The four Japanese turned out to be engineers from Satake who were supervising production for her, thereby doubling their firm's insurance on its money. Her assistant turned out to be one of the still relatively small number of Vietnamese from the wrong side of the political tracks who were being given a place in the society if they had skills useful to those who ran the country.

He was at first extremely reticent about his background. He relaxed somewhat as the morning went on and we toured the plant. He was actually fluent in three foreign languages, having taken his *baccalauréat* in French from the best lycée in old Saigon, Jean-Jacques Rousseau, now a Vietnamese high school. He had then escaped the war in the way the sons of formerly well-to-do Saigon families had, by obtaining an exit visa to study overseas. He had received his bachelor's degree at Sophia University in Tokyo and had subsequently spent two years at the Georgetown University School of Foreign Service in Washington, D.C. Bad luck had brought him home in 1974. He was thirty-seven years old, and he now had his first good job since the collapse in 1975 because Mrs. Thi had a need for his languages. He made it clear that he did not want to see us afterward outside of her presence, and he would not relax enough to give us his full name, only his first. But would we say hello to a prominent academic in Washington who would remember him by it?

When we encountered others like him, the pattern was the same. At Vung Tau, Saigon's weekend beach resort at the tip of Cap Saint-Jacques on the South China Sea, forty miles to the east—a nascent oil town too these days because of offshore drilling—there was a new clinic that was a showcase of Vietnamese-American friendship. A group of American veterans had raised money to pay for the construction materials and then come to Vietnam and raised the building itself in joint labor with Vietnamese veterans they might once have faced on the battlefield. Carved into the black marble of the dedicatory plaque were two clasped hands, on the wrist of one the Stars and Stripes, on the wrist of the other the star of the Ho Chi Minh flag.

The clinic director was a surgeon who also spoke excellent English. He had spent six years in one of the grimmest of the "reeducation camps," in a wild area of the Central Highlands where the borders of Vietnam, Laos, and Cambodia meet, because he had been a senior medical officer in the ARVN, deputy director of the main military hospital. After his release he had earned his living in Vung Tau as a lowly technician in a local clinic nearby. Then the Vietnam veterans' group had appeared. "You know how to deal with the Americans," he had been told, and he had been put in charge. He was a modest man who rode a secondhand bicycle.

At one of the better hospitals serving the Saigon area the head of the department of internal medicine was a former ARVN doctor who had spent two years in a camp. He had had to switch from general surgery to internal medicine in order to find employment, but he was prospering at last and wore nice slacks and fancy loafers. He made the typical Saigonese comment on the privatization of medical care and the other changes taking place under *doi moi.* "We're marching backward," he said in French.

For every case like these there were many thousands of other losers with scant hope. North of Cap Saint-Jacques is a stretch of beach called Long Hai, one of the most beautiful in Vietnam. I wanted to drive there because during the war it had always been too dangerous to go farther down the beach than a curve where some rocky hills descend to the sea in a point—the guerrillas had owned the solitude of the beach beyond. After we had rounded the forbidden curve and passed several miles of relatively unspoiled shore, solitude was suddenly gone in another confrontation with Vietnam's burgeoning population—a new hamlet of thousands of people, living in thatched huts on the sand and cooking their evening meal in the spectacle of the beach at sunset.

A middle-aged man in shirt and shorts stepped out of the crowd that gathered around us and recited in perfect English the last names of the U.S. Army captains and majors for whom he had worked. Did I know any of them and where they lived? He wanted help to get to the United States. He said that for nine years he had been a driver at an Army ammunition dump near Saigon and had paid for his services to the U.S. government with three years of mild reeducation in his home village. He and his wife had drifted to this hamlet of squatters a couple of years earlier in search of a livelihood. They were cooking and selling noodle soup, doing about as well as their neighbors who had not worked for the Americans and who scraped by with fishing, shrimping, and laboring in a village center farther down the road. I took his name and told him how to apply to emigrate.

The most heartrending cases were the homeless ARVN veterans with missing arms and legs who wandered the Saigon streets on crutches, begging. The lack of production facilities within the country and the failure of the U.S. government to carry through with its promises of assistance to the disabled had left amputees from both sides without prosthetic devices, but those who lost limbs for Ho Chi Minh usually had a place to lie down at night.

Nguyen Phi Tuyen of the Ho Chi Minh City Service of External Relations, who ran the Vietnamese side of the Orderly Departure Program, the legal way to leave the country, said Vietnam's policy was to allow all of the 94,000 former Saigon government officials and military officers released from reeducation camps, as well as their dependents—roughly half a million people—to emigrate if they wished to do so. There was no doubt that most would leave if they could. (Only about 120 persons—eight generals, twelve colonels, ex-C.I.A. agents, and police and security types who had worked in interrogation centers where torture was common—continued to be imprisoned at the last reeducation camp near Ham Tan, northeast of Saigon. The Minister of the Interior when we were in Vietnam, Mai Chi Tho, a younger brother of Le Duc Tho, said they were still being held because they were "the most dangerous." They had allegedly committed "terrible crimes" and "their thinking hasn't changed," he said. "If they would admit what they've done, they'd be released." He defended confining the 120 men as preferable to putting them on trial. If they had been tried, "some might have been executed once or twice or several times because of their guilt," he said.)

Washington has so far agreed to take, with some exceptions, only those who spent three years or more in a reeducation camp, an estimated 145,000 persons when their dependents are included, under a special refugee program. Tuyen argued that the United States was morally obligated to accept the entire 94,000 and their families; it had stigmatized their lives by encouraging them to take the American side. He said Vietnam also feared the addition to its social problems of a large group of people in a permanent limbo. He argued that once some were accepted, all would pin their hopes on emigration, regardless of how realistic the possibility was, and never settle into permanent work and living patterns.

Unstated by Tuyen and other officials was the desire of Vietnam to rid itself of a minority relegated to the end of the line in a country that had no jobs anyway for a fourth of its unstigmatized citizens; a minority who also would never reconcile themselves to the outcome of the war because the one thing the years of confessing and lecture listening and supposedly "cleansing" manual labor in the camps had not done was change their minds.

The park behind the Roman Catholic cathedral in the center of the city has been unofficially named "Reeducation Park." The grassy expanse faces the External Relations Service building, once the Foreign Ministry of the Saigon regime. Every day, three weeks out of the month, American ODP officers from the U.S. Embassy in Bangkok sit in offices assigned to them at the back of the building interviewing applicants for immigration. The ex–civil servants and former ARVN captains and majors and lieutenant colonels gather in the park.

For some, material want is not the worst problem. The fortunate ones live considerably better than the poor in the North, on remittances from relatives who have already made it to the United States in the flight just before the fall in 1975, or since then by boat or through the ODP. They gossip to pass the time, and they hope. Having tied their destinies to the great foreign power during the war, they wait for it to rescue them. The wait is apparently going to be a long one. By the spring of 1992, the United States had admitted about 45,000 of the estimated 145,000 former reeducation camp inmates and their dependents who qualified under the three-year rule. There was no indication Washington was going to relax the rule for the other 350,000.

Not all of the losers had been on the Saigon side. The one place I was asked *not* to go in Saigon was a house at 24/1 Truong Dinh Street that was the headquarters of the Club of Former Resistance Fighters. Nobody forbade me to go, but I could see that if I did I would get Thang and Tien into trouble and also embarrass the officials at the Service of External Relations, who were otherwise trying to be helpful. The losers who gathered at Truong Dinh Street and at the branches of the club in the eighteen districts of

Ho Chi Minh City were the losers the authorities really worried about. They had that standing no ex-ARVN officer could ever possess. While several of the members were retired generals, the more representative were the lower-ranking men and women who had fought and suffered and now found themselves with little but their self-respect in the poverty of a bleak peace. What differentiated them from so many others like them elsewhere in the country was that they were articulate people who lived in a place where the ferment of independent thinking had led to such acts as the formation of their club.

It was, of course, not necessary to go to Truong Dinh Street to hear members speak of the disillusionment that had led them to form the club. "We spent our lives to have a Vietnam that was independent, free, and with happiness for everyone," a retired major who was active in the organization said over lunch. "Now we have independence but not happiness. The bureaucrats have the cars and the franchises, the mutilated are poor and have nothing."

The major was in his late sixties, in frail health, and unable to exist on his pension. His wife worked as a seamstress to help support them. He had prosperous relatives in the United States; his pride would not let him turn to them for money because they had split over the war. A former lycée classmate and friend who had once been on the Saigon side but then drifted leftward after emigrating to the United States in the early 1960s discovered during a visit to Vietnam that the major was going blind from cataracts in both eyes. The military hospital, where he was theoretically entitled to free care, no longer had the facilities for such surgery, and the major could not afford a private doctor. The lycée classmate hired an eye surgeon to remove the cataracts.

The club claimed to have thousands of members in the Ho Chi Minh City area. Eligibility was not confined to retired military personnel. Any man or woman who could prove that he or she had participated in the resistance against the French or the Americans, as a member of the underground civil administration, a teacher, a medical worker, a labor union organizer—in any capacity—could join. The club even had an overseas member, a Frenchman who had been jailed by the Thieu regime for displaying a Viet Cong flag while a lycée teacher in Saigon.

After the first two issues were seized, the club had given up publishing a newspaper. It had applied to the Politburo and the National Assembly for a charter to form a national federation. The major was certain that if permission were granted the club would rapidly acquire hundreds of thousands of members all over the country. The response of the authorities had been to create a separate government-sponsored national veterans' association to try to coopt the veterans' movement. In a society where a war record confers a certain immunity along with respect, an independent national veterans' federation would pose a serious challenge to the monopoly on political power held by the Vietnamese Communist Party.

Democracy has not fared well in Southeast Asia. The Vietnamese have no democratic models among their immediate neighbors to which they can look. Thailand is a right-wing state ruled by its military; Singapore, a civilian dictatorship under Lee Kuan Yew. The Filipino oligarchy pretends to honor democratic forms in an archipelago where chaos reigns amidst guerrillas and private armies. Nor do the Vietnamese have democratic antecedents in their history. Rather, the Communist Party, with its hierarchy and ritual, has become a kind of modern counterpart of the Confucian mandarinate that governed the country under the emperors before the arrival of the French.

Nguyen Van Linh and those who think like him believe that Vietnam can create prosperity through economic liberalism and escape political instability by maintaining the dominance of the Communist Party. The retired major who belonged to the Club of Former Resistance Fighters is also a forty-year veteran of the Party. "We are not discontented with socialism and the Party but with the distortions and errors," he said. "We want a true socialism. We want a Communist Party that is powerful and capable and that represents the people and the spirit of the country."

Most Americans see a contradiction between economic liberalism and one-party politics. Most of the Vietnamese who won the war see the issue in a different perspective. They say they want a society ruled by law, not whimsy, public officials held to account, corruption checked, and more of what Mr. Linh called "the democratization of social life" in cultural and political freedoms. How the Vietnamese are going to achieve these desires in the conditions they have inherited is a dilemma they will have to resolve in their own way.

My friend Ly Tong Ba had been one of the losers on the Saigon side. He had not run away in 1975 and had spent twelve years and eight months in captivity and reeducation camps. We had met in the Mekong delta in 1962. Ba was a captain then, commanding a company of armored personnel carriers attached to the 7th ARVN Infantry Division, the division responsible for the northern half of the delta. John Vann was its senior advisor. I was in my first year in Vietnam as a reporter for United Press International. We had shared days of fighting in the hamlets and rice paddies and the urban political upheavals of the early sixties. Whenever there was a coup d'état, the plotting generals would inevitably order Ba and his armor to Saigon to help them prevail. He and I had a standing appointment to meet the morning after each coup at a French café called Brodard's. Over bracing dark coffee Ba would tell me what he knew of the inside story.

Ba had been a favorite of the American advisors because, while few ARVN officers ever fully satisfied the U.S. Army's model of aggressiveness, Ba would fight and he was not a crook. His house in Saigon was comfortable, with modern plumbing and air-conditioning, but modest by the standards of his contemporaries. He never owned a Mercedes-Benz, settling for an older Peugeot staff car and a civilian jeep he painted white.

At the time of the North Vietnamese Army offensive in the spring of 1972, Ba was a full colonel commanding an infantry division in the mountains of the Central Highlands. John Vann had maneuvered him into the job after becoming senior American officer for the Highlands and the adjacent Central Coast. When the Communists struck their usual surprise opening blows, the other ARVN commanders in the Highlands either ran—despite Vann cursing them to fight—or wanted to run. Ba agreed to stay and try to hold the key town of Kontum. Vann promised him round-the-clock strikes by the B-52s and plenty of U.S. fighter-bomber and helicopter support.

It was still nip and tuck, but Ba held his division together and helped win a major victory at Kontum that turned back the offensive, saved the Nixon administration from the embarrassment of a rout, and staved off the collapse of the Saigon regime for another three years. Thieu rewarded him with promotion to one-star general. Soon after, the crisis was past and Vann had been killed in a helicopter crash, however, Thieu took the division away from Ba because he would not cooperate in corruption with a new corps commander. When I had last seen him in 1973, Ba had been in an administrative job in Saigon as chief of the armor branch.

I found him through his former enemies. The address I had obtained for him before leaving the United States, the one in the files of the U.S. side of the ODP program, turned out to be incorrect. The people at that address, a working-class suburb on the northeast side of the city, seemed pleased to see visiting Americans, but they knew nothing of an ARVN general named Ly Tong Ba. Trinh Van Anh, chief press officer for the Ho Chi Minh City Service of External Relations, got me the correct address, another working-class neighborhood, this time in the Chinese section of Cholon.

Ba was living with one of his sisters and the sister's daughter and her family, all crowded into a one-room apartment on the second floor with a curtained-off sleeping area for the young woman and her children. The toilet was down some rough concrete stairs to the rear of the first-floor apartment, where the landlord, a former Viet Cong, lived in similarly crowded quarters with his family. The landlord had the certificate of the Order of Liberation proudly displayed on a wall. Ba wasn't home on the evening we came. He was off visiting some ex-comrades, other former reeducation camp inmates. Susan and I talked with his sister in her long-unused French while one of Ba's nephews went in search of him, but when he didn't appear in a couple of hours we returned to the Rex Hotel for a late dinner. I got a phone call from the lobby. It was Ba. He came up and had a steak. We reminisced, and the next night Susan and I went back to the apartment to hear his story.

Toward the end Thieu had apparently become desperate enough to let corruption take a backseat. In December 1974 he gave Ba command of the 25th ARVN Infantry Division, deployed then at Tay Ninh, fifty-five miles northwest of Saigon. The ARVN forces were on their own; there was no longer an American advisor standing beside the radio to summon B-52s and fighter-bombers. The last of the American forces had withdrawn the better part of two years earlier under the Paris Agreement. On March 10, 1975, the Vietnamese Communists loosed their offensive with a surprise assault on the town of Ban Me Thuot in the lower Central Highlands, seizing the town immediately and scattering the reserves dispatched by helicopter to retake it.

Thieu panicked and started issuing unrealistic and contradictory orders. Ba wanted to pull his division back to the former base of the U.S. 25th Infantry Division, near Cu Chi District center, closer to Saigon, and with other ARVN divisions form a defensive belt around the city. Their slim and only hope, Ba argued, was "to bring the tiger out of the jungle and kill him"—to try to entice the NVA into fighting on the ARVN's terms. They would have to repeat on a larger scale the defensive success at Kontum, despite the fact that they now lacked the critical component of American air power. Thieu wouldn't hear of it. He wanted Ba to attack north toward the Highlands. Ba replied that the maneuver would be difficult even for a U.S. Army division; it would be absolute folly for the 25th ARVN. The tiger would devour them. "We will lose the whole Twenty-fifth. We will lose the whole game. We will lose maybe Saigon," he told his president.

In the meantime Thieu set off an enormous debacle by ordering his generals to abandon the Highlands and the former imperial capital of Hue in I Corps farther north. Thousands perished as the ARVN troops fled pell-mell, disintegrating faster than the NVA could catch up with them. Yet Ba still could not get permission from Thieu to withdraw from Tay Ninh. By the time he received permission in late April the NVA had caught up and were around and behind him; he had to fight his way back to Cu Chi. All he managed to get through to the former U.S. base were his reconnaissance company, a couple of battalions of infantry, and a platoon of tanks.

At five P.M. on April 28 they were bombed by planes from their own air force. Three A-37 jets tried to knock out Ba's command post in the old American bunker. The pilots had defected after they and their aircraft were captured by the advancing North Vietnamese. The air raid was another signal that Gen. Van Tien Dung and his commanders were clearing away the last obstacles for an assault on Saigon itself. The Communist artillery opened next with a terrifying barrage, and then the NVA commandos struck. Ba's remnant fought into the night and through the morning of the twenty-ninth. Early that afternoon he decided they had to break out and reorganize at Hoc Mon, ten miles farther south, near the edge of the city. Retreat proved impossible; the men had lost heart. They ran through the main gate of the base in a rabble, ignoring Ba's shouts to stop, jostling him aside despite his rank.

Within an hour Ly Tong Ba, general of the ARVN, was lying on his back under the water of a flooded rice paddy, trying to poke only his nose above the surface in order to breathe without being seen. He had learned the trick from the Viet Cong: The guerrillas had used it in the Mekong delta to escape his armored carriers. He had just one soldier left—his bodyguard, who was lying beside him. Ba had managed to gather his staff and the division reconnaissance company and set off for Hoc Mon by foot, but his enemies had anticipated this move too and had been waiting in ambush along the road. "Shoot back!" Ba had yelled when the ambushers opened fire. No one obeyed him. "We lose now, General," one of his staff captains said and then, like the others, obeyed the Communist soldiers who called to them with portable, battery-powered loudspeakers to drop their weapons and surrender.

In a couple of hours, everything seemed quiet. Ba lifted his head out of the paddy water, then slowly stood up. The Communist soldiers had left with their captives. "We were two lonely men—I and my bodyguard," he said. They stripped off their uniforms and changed into the escape garb Ba had brought for such an eventuality—the black pajama work clothes of a Vietnamese peasant. It was about five P.M. Ba explained to his bodyguard that they would lie in the paddy until dark and then slip away to Saigon.

He had to get back to Saigon to save his family because the Americans had also let him down. He felt angry and betrayed. Four days earlier, when he could still use the helicopter assigned to a division commander, he had flown to Saigon from Cu Chi and gone to the U.S. Embassy to see a man he had every reason to believe would help him—Charles Timmes, a retired U.S. Army general who was working for the CIA. They had met at the beginning of the 1960s, when Timmes was a major general commanding the original U.S. Military Assistance and Advisory Group (MAAG) in South Vietnam and Ba was still a captain.

An outgoing, informal fighting man who had won a Distinguished Service Cross jumping into Normandy on D-Day at the head of a paratroop battalion, "Charlie" Timmes had struck up friendships with Ba and a host of other ARVN officers. In 1967, after he had retired from the Army, the CIA had persuaded him to return to Vietnam on its payroll as a special liaison agent to the South Vietnamese military. For all the years between that time and the end that was now approaching, Timmes had battened off those friendships to glean information for the U.S. government. Yet Ba had not merely seen Timmes as a CIA agent with influence. Because of the circumstances of their first meeting—general to captain—and the way the relationship had persisted since, Ba had regarded Timmes as a kind of father figure, a lineal representative of the U.S. Army and of John Vann and the other American advisors he had fought a war with down through the years.

Ba told Timmes that he was going to stay with his troops, but he wanted his wife and children and several close relatives evacuated to the United States. He handed Timmes a list he had composed with names and addresses and phone numbers. Timmes hesitated. The Charlie Timmes who had leapt out the open doorway of a C-47 into the predawn darkness over Normandy in 1944 wasn't the same man who had hung around Vietnam until 1975 because he liked the country and enjoyed the excitement of the war. He had grown accustomed to using other men rather than leading them, and he had acquired the fecklessness of the bureaucrat.

"Well, it's very difficult now, Ba," he said. "The evacuation flights are very crowded." He made excuses about being busy. Ba was stunned. At Saumur in the Loire Valley, where he had gone to attend an armored cavalry course in the 1950s, the French officers had talked of duty and a soldier's code. He had heard the same phrases in a different language at the Armor School at Fort Knox, Kentucky, where the U.S. Army had later sent him. He was behaving with honor. He was not deserting his post. Yet this man he had admired and trusted, who could have his family evacuated by picking up the telephone, was deserting him. He kept himself under control and got up to go. Timmes said he would do what he could.

Ba knew Timmes hadn't done anything because his wife had managed to get through on the phone to his Cu Chi command bunkèr from their house in Saigon that morning of the twenty-ninth and asked for advice. "Wife, take an initiative—I'm fighting now," Ba said. Then the phone line went dead. As he lay in the mud-gray water of the paddy, he could see an American plane overhead. He wished he had a radio to call to it for help. He could not know that the plane was one of many fighter-bombers protecting Navy and Marine helicopters from the Seventh Fleet that were conducting a massive last-minute evacuation of Saigon. Approximately seven thousand people, most of them Vietnamese, were lifted out before the NVA tanks burst into the city on the morning of the thirtieth. Ba's family was not among them.

Darkness brought a glow in the sky to the southeast: Tan Son Nhut Air Base was burning from the North Vietnamese artillery shells. Ba and his lone soldier welcomed the fires. They intended to use the glow as a beacon to guide them to the city. First, however, they had to get across the river and the bridge didn't belong to their army anymore. They could hear local Viet Cong guerrillas standing on it calling to the troops in a nearby ARVN post to surrender. They stripped off their boots to swim to the other side, with Ba leading the way.

Somehow they ended up back on the same bank. It started raining hard, and the clouds obliterated the glow of the fires at Tan Son Nhut. They got lost. Ba had forgotten to bring a compass, and his bodyguard's compass had been ruined by the paddy water. They lay down in a cemetery to sleep for a while, Ba on top of one of the tombs, his bodyguard on the ground beside him, then wandered some more until Ba grew too exhausted to continue. Their boots were gone now, and one of Ba's feet ached from a wound. During the fighting earlier in the day a piece of shrapnel or some jagged object had sliced into it.

Ba decided they would wait until daybreak and then hire a Lambretta, a three-wheel minibus common in the countryside, to drive them to Saigon. At dawn on the thirtieth, as the last of the evacuation helicopters was lifting off from the roof of the U.S. Embassy in the city, they crossed a rice paddy and were about to enter a hamlet when a voice shouted "Halt!" A teenage farm boy stepped out of the trees with an AK-47 assault rifle leveled at them. The young guerrilla had obviously been watching them.

"Finished," Ba's bodyguard said. Ba had a pistol in a pocket of his black pajamas. To try to use it would only get them killed. He tossed it into the paddy water, stripping off his gold Omega watch because he didn't want his enemies to have it and tossing it away too. Ba had never risen beyond one-star general. Despite his faithfulness, Thieu had not rewarded him with a second star after giving him the 25th. Nevertheless, when Ba had changed into the black pajamas, he had carefully detached the single silver star from each of his uniform collar tabs and placed them in a pocket. The stars followed the pistol and the gold Omega watch into the mire.

He was certain he would be shot. His certainty of execution increased when he found himself by the afternoon of his captivity transported back to his Cu Chi base, now the headquarters of the 320th North Vietnamese Army Division. The 320th was one of two NVA divisions he had helped to defeat at Kontum in 1972.

Along with John Vann and his other American mentors, he was responsible for killing thousands of NVA soldiers there. One day just before the end of that battle the voice of a man who was apparently a senior NVA officer broke into a radio conversation and urged Ba to cease being a "tool of the imperialists" and come over to "the side of the people." Ba had taunted the man. "You're losing, so now you want to talk," he said. "You hardheaded son of a bitch, you're one of the first we'll shoot when we win the revolution," the voice replied.

On the afternoon of May 1, he and five of his senior staff officers, who had also been captured and were being held with him, were loaded into a Lambretta and taken to a house near the market in Cu Chi town. A fine meal of two chickens, rice, and other fixings awaited them on the table. They were told to sit down and eat. Ba had not eaten for two days. Assuming that the delicious-looking chicken was a last meal for condemned men, he sat down as ordered but refused to eat. The others did. Ba regretted his decision late that night back in the darkness of the bunker at the base where he and his staff officers were being imprisoned. He was getting hungrier and there was no indication precisely when he would be shot.

Suddenly the door of the bunker opened and a voice called for Ly Tong Ba to come out. "Follow the man with the flashlight," the voice said as Ba stepped into the night. He did as he was told. The armed man who had given the command and several others fell in behind him. Ba wondered what the bullet would feel like when it hit him in the head. Would they tie him up before they raised the muzzle to his skull? The flashlight led him to a small building where two uniformed men were sitting at a table illuminated by a kerosene lantern. Ba assumed they were NVA officers because they had envelope-style briefcases for maps and documents. "Sit down, General," one of them said. Good, they want to talk, I won't be shot for a while, Ba thought. Did he have any troops hidden in the area? one of the officers asked. "No, I'm the last troop," Ba said. Was he sure? Yes, he was sure.

A large glass of tea was placed in front of him, and they slid paper and pen across the table and told him to write out his curriculum vitae. He looked at the tea and decided it was probably poisoned. He was thirsty as well as hungry. "Let's finish life with tea," he said to himself and emptied the glass in a gulp. "General, you're thirsty," one of the officers said and got him another glass. He drank that too at a gulp.

The tea was sweet with lots of sugar and tasted marvelous. Over the next half hour, as he wrote an outline of his family history and career, he waited for the poison to take effect. His father, a sergeant major in France's pre–World War II native forces, had chosen his side for him in this war by sending him to a lycée in Can Tho and then to the French Army school for the sons of colonial soldiers at Vung Tau. From there he had gone to the new academy for Vietnamese officers at Dalat, graduating in 1952 with distinction. Ba had never doubted the correctness of the choice. As he was led back to the bunker, he was still sure that he would soon be shot, but he felt better for the tea.

He spent his first year of "reeducation" with twenty-seven other Saigon generals in a large barracks room at the former ARVN training center at Hoc Mon. When he was driven there in a night jeep ride a month and a half after being captured, he believed for the first time that he probably would live—and if not: "At least I won't be shot alone; we'll be shot together." There were some killings, local vendetta executions by men and women who had waited years to settle scores and refused to be denied vengeance by the policy of higher authority. Right after his capture Ba had briefly been kept with the Saigon district chief for Cu Chi. The district chief had wanted to be sent to the 320th Division headquarters with Ba. His enemy counterpart, the local Viet Cong district chief, had showed up and said, "No, you stay and have supper with me tonight." The man had disappeared.

The previous month and a half had not been reassuring for Ba. The solitary bit of good news had been that his wife and children had escaped by boat to Malaysia. His sister had told him. She had pleaded in tears with an NVA guard at the Cu Chi base until he felt sorry for her and let her inside. Ba couldn't help breaking down and weeping himself when he saw her. He had been shifted from the bunker where he was initially confined to a chicken coop. His troops from the 25th, who were only loosely held and were allowed to go into the town to buy food, had tossed him beer and bread over the wire and penicillin tablets for his wounded foot. He had then been placed under guard in a Cu Chi barracks. A Polish filmmaker had appeared one day, and Ba and his staff had been forced to fake a surrender to NVA troops in their former command post bunker. Ba subsequently saw the film and was told that the Pole received a gold medal in Warsaw for his "newsreel."

His wife had taken his advice to act on her own initiative. She heard a rumor the day after the fall of Saigon that he had been killed in the fighting at Cu Chi. The driver at his house remained faithful and stayed with her. Two days later, because there was no further word of Ba's fate, she loaded herself and their three children, her mother, a brother who was also an ARVN officer, and his wife into Ba's white jeep and had the driver take them to Go Cong near the coast southeast of the city. There she parted with all of her jewelry and her cash savings, several million piastres, to pay a fisherman to sail them to Malaysia. Part of the agreement was that the fisherman would return to Vietnam and smuggle Ba to Malaysia as well if it turned out that he was alive. The fisherman kept the bargain, sailing back to Vietnam in a couple of months, but smuggled somebody else to Malaysia when he learned from Ba's sister that Ba was imprisoned. Ba's house was looted and then occupied by the families of Viet Cong.

The Vietnamese Communists thought at first that they really could change minds. Ba and his twenty-seven fellow ARVN generals kept at Hoc Mon were subjected to a carefully structured course taught by a cadre of teachers who had prepared for their task. (The instructors were called "cadres," the universal Vietnamese Communist term for an officer or an official or specialist.) The generals were given neatly printed booklets to read on such subjects as colonialism and imperialism. They had to ponder what they read, write essays, and discuss their thoughts and conclusions in classes led by the cadres. If anyone's comments did not accurately reflect the printed texts and supplementary lectures by the cadres, the others were instigated to criticize the delinquent student. They slept on cots in the same barracks room where they received their lessons, never allowed out of it except for daily physical exercise breaks in a barbed-wire enclosed walkway and trips to the toilet and shower.

Although visits and letters were forbidden, the cadres kept in touch with the families and informed them when packets of medicine and other items such as clothing could be sent. At Tet, the holiday that for the Vietnamese is Thanksgiving, Christmas, and New Year's rolled into one, the cadres solicited taped messages with family news that they played for each prisoner. Ba's sister made one for him. Some of the generals studied hard, thinking that if they learned well they would be released. While Ba lost his fear of being executed, he was skeptical that academic excellence mattered. He assumed he would be held for the rest of his life.

The fear returned suddenly one morning in the predawn darkness. The generals were roused at four A.M., made to pack their few belongings in a hurry, then marched outside and ordered to climb into the back of a canvas-covered army truck. Some thought they would be driven to Cambodia and handed over to the Khmer Rouge for torture and gruesome execution. Instead, they were driven to Tan Son Nhut and flown to Yen Bai, northwest of Hanoi, for the next phase of their education—manual labor.

A hammer striking a sheet of steel hung from a wire—the camp bell—woke them in their mountain valley at five-thirty in the morning. Only the main sleeping barracks had been erected before their arrival. They had to build everything else from scratch, dig a well, and grow food for themselves by planting vegetable gardens in the valley and clearing fields for manioc on the surrounding mountain slopes. Digging up the wild bamboo on the slopes with crowbars was grueling work. The trees they also cleared had to be chopped into firewood for cooking and carried back down to the camp. Ba's knees ached from the strain of the heavy loads on the steep inclines. If anyone shirked by lightening his load, he would be singled out and criticized that night after the evening meal by the cadres and his fellow prisoners. The beds they then lay down on were homemade bamboo platforms with a reed mat on top.

At first they were fed adequately—three to four bowls of rice at noon and again in the evening, with *nuoc mam*, a fermented fish sauce that is a source of vitamins, and occasional vegetables and bits of meat. In a few months the ration was cut to two bowls twice a day (breakfast was just tea, which a rotating prisoner crew who rose at four A.M. prepared), and they went hungry, sometimes eating grass for vitamins, until they could harvest the manioc and their patches of water lilies, onions, potatoes, and cabbage. They had no fertilizer for the vegetables and had to use their own night soil, which they collected and spread in its immense stench. Two of the generals perished. One, a police general who was a diabetic, died slowly from lack of insulin. The other, the former commander of the ARVN Special Forces, developed serious stomach trouble, was sent to a hospital for surgery, and then died of a heart attack after his return to the camp.

Ba, who is physically sturdy and the kind of outgoing person who craves something to do, was not adversely affected by the two years at Yen Bai. The winters in the North, when the temperature hangs in the 40s and it rains constantly, were hard because he was not accustomed to them. His sister, who suspected he might end up there, had sent him a wool shirt while he was still at Hoc Mon and a thermos to hold hot water for tea when he was cold or sick. The cadres also distributed old but serviceable army field jackets with cotton padding and extra blankets.

The next phase of Ba's imprisonment, five years of monotonous confinement, was much more difficult to bear. It began in 1978 as the border fighting with the Khmer Rouge grew more violent and Vietnam's relations with China became increasingly embittered. The Communist leadership decided that their defeated enemies were another potential fifth column and had to be placed under close watch. The generals were trucked to Ha Dong, just southwest of Hanoi, and jailed in a compound of small brick buildings with barred windows that Ba thinks were originally built for captured American pilots. What started as a wartime measure then acquired a bureaucratic inertia, years drifted by, and the experiment at changing minds degenerated into simple punishment.

The buildings had electric lights and toilets nearby, and their tile roofs didn't leak when it rained. The generals were allowed a six-and-a-half-pound package of food and medicine every third month. Ba's wife, who had settled in Las Vegas with their children after being granted a refugee visa to the United States, faithfully sent money and care packets to Saigon, so that his package would be filled with dried soups and other dehydrated foods, vitamins, and antibiotics. Letters started to come, and a few of the generals (Ba was not one) were even permitted family visits.

None of these comforts mattered. The men were held half a dozen to a brick building. Their only exercise, except for calisthenics some disciplined themselves to do inside, were trips to the toilet. "The worst thing about it was that we never knew when we would get out," Ba said. His weight slid to about 115 pounds, down 45 pounds from the 160 he had weighed at the time he was captured. A clandestine photograph taken during a visit by another general's family shows him as a wraith.

In 1983 the generals were moved once more, this time to a large camp near Phu Ly in the Red River delta south of Hanoi, where several thousand other Saigon officers and officials still in captivity were being kept. Once again the generals all slept together in one building. They refused to work as they had at Yen Bai, saying that some of them were too old for hard labor. The cadres were initially angry, but then agreed to let them perform light chores and grow their own gardens. Ba puttered at his and also raised two chickens and a duck for eggs. Others bred rabbits. On Sundays the prisoners invited the cadres to songfests and picnics of chicken.

A new commandant became fearful the inmates were subverting their keepers and forbade them to raise any more chickens, but did not ban the purchase of chickens for imminent consumption with money the men received from their families during visits. Ba's sister came up to see him. The prisoners noticed that they had much better access to antibiotics, through their packages, than the cadres did and gave the cadres antibiotics for their sick children. Ba read a lot—the Hanoi newspapers, books of Chinese poetry, medical texts, an English-language Soviet magazine, anything he could get his hands on that was not Marxist-Leninist jargon.

In 1987 and 1988, with Nguyen Van Linh the new general secretary of the Party and *doi moi* well under way, the Phu Ly camp was gradually dissolved through large-scale releases. In mid-December 1987 Ba was given a train ticket from Hanoi to Saigon. His sister nursed him back to health, taking him on trips to the mountain resort of Da Lat and sightseeing in Phnom Penh, at the time still occupied by the Vietnamese.

By the time I saw him in the summer of 1989 he was back up to 150 pounds and looked fit for his fifty-eight years and spiffy in a navy blue Lacoste shirt. A tennis racket stood in a corner of the one-room apartment. Ba played frequently at Saigon's once-exclusive Cercle Sportif. The place had been declared a public recreation center after 1975 and, like much else in a country that lacks funds for public facilities, was now dirty and run-down, but Ba joked that the tennis courts still had nets. He had a minor eye problem amenable to surgery and was going to do something about it after he got to the United States. He was waiting for the authorities in Hanoi to grant him an exit permit. His name was already on the list of those former reeducation camp prisoners acceptable to the U.S. government.

Not long after Ba's release and return to Saigon, a visiting American television correspondent asked to interview a prominent veteran of the camps. The Ho Chi Minh City press office volunteered Ba. "What am I supposed to say?" Ba asked a couple of Vietnamese security officers who showed up at the interview. "Say what you think," they replied. The reporter asked Ba if he had been "reeducated" during the twelve years and eight months. "Still not now and never will be a Communist," Ba replied. Had he been well treated? "Well, it was still a prison . . . not an R and R camp," Ba said. (R and R is a U.S. military term for rest and recreation.)

The night lengthened in the crowded, grubby apartment as Ba told me his story. One of his sister's grandchildren, feverish and vomiting, whimpered in the curtained-off sleeping area. I asked him if he regretted his decision to stay until the end. A number of his fellow Saigon generals had deserted their troops and run just before the collapse, and most of those who were with him in captivity had been caught because they had missed an American evacuation helicopter on the last day. "I'm glad I didn't run away in 1975. A real soldier doesn't run away," Ba said. On January 19, 1990, Ly Tong Ba boarded a plane at Tan Son Nhut and, after a brief stay at the immigration-processing center in Bangkok, joined his family in Las Vegas.

On January 2, 1963, at a place called Ap Bac in the Mekong Delta, where Ba was then a captain commanding a company of armored personnel carriers, the Viet Cong had also not run away. For the first time in the war three hundred and fifty of the elusive guerrillas had stood their ground and fought all day against Saigon troops four times their number equipped with artillery and Ba's armor and supported by American helicopters and fighter-bombers. With just grenades and the captured rifles, machine guns, and other infantry arms they held in their hands the Viet Cong had killed and wounded approximately two hundred of their opponents, including three Americans dead; shot down five helicopters; and stopped Ba's armored machines despite the lack of a single antitank weapon. The battle had been a turning point. From that day forward the "raggedy-ass little bastards," as the American generals had mocked them, had grown into a powerful army that by 1965 was on the verge of total victory in the South, forcing Lyndon Johnson to intervene with the regular divisions of the U.S. Army and the Marine Corps to rescue Washington's protégés in Saigon.

A quarter of a century later there was a billboard where the dirt road toward the former battleground turned off the hardtop of the main delta highway. The art section of the province staff had painted a scene of a helicopter in flames, an armored personnel carrier blowing up, and an ARVN parachute battalion descending in a fruitless attempt at rescue, a reasonable if not entirely accurate portrayal of the violence on that memorable day.

Like Ben Suc, Ap Bac and its four neighboring hamlets (the

word "Ap" means hamlet) in the village of Tan Phu had to be
redeemed by the inhabitants who returned in 1975 from the empty
ruin of charred homes and brush-grown rice fields that was the
heritage the American war bequeathed to so much of the South
Vietnamese countryside. The French-American historian Bernard
Fall, who was killed while reporting the war in the South in 1967,
liked to quote a line from Tacitus to describe the culmination of
the relentless round of bombs and shells and defoliants: "Where
they make a desert, they call it peace." The process of clearing and
rebuilding, with its attendant horror of people killed and wounded
by unexploded grenades and other ordnance, had then been set
back by a severe typhoon that struck the area in 1978. Among the
casualties were virtually all of the newly planted fruit trees, blown
away or drowned in the flooding.

In contrast to the surprise visit to Ben Suc, when no one was
waiting, I had prearranged the trip to Ap Bac, and an assemblage
of village officials, veterans, and the ever-inquisitive Vietnamese
children were gathered at the new village council house, finally
completed in 1985.

As at Ben Suc, the village was run by those who had resisted.
Tran Van Hy, chairman of the People's Committee, lost his father,
a sister, and a nephew during the battle. They were killed by
shrapnel from a bomb or an artillery shell while hiding in a pile of
straw. Two other nephews with them were wounded. Mr. Hy was
fifteen at the time and ran messages for the guerrillas. During the
chaos he had to bury his father and sister in a neighboring village
and wasn't able to properly inter their remains in the family
graveyard until after 1975. Le Van Vy, the Party secretary of the
village, had been the guerrilla youth leader in the hamlet just above
Ap Bac. He had distributed food and ammunition to the fighters
and carried away wounded. Pinned to a Vietnamese flag on one of
the walls of the council house were the three high decorations the
village had been awarded. Above the flag was a portrait of Ho Chi
Minh, before it a vase of flowers.

Valor had not brought material reward. There wasn't enough
land to go around, and the land wasn't as productive as it ought

to have been. The postwar village had approximately 5,000 inhabitants in 1,005 families, but only 1,310 acres of rice land and
another 428 acres of less fertile ground suitable for vegetables and
fruit trees. Mr. Vy, the Party secretary, explained that unlike
conditions in more fortunate neighboring villages, much of Tan
Phu's rice land was too high for easy flooding and had a salinity
problem as well. The farmers were also caught in the classic
squeeze between the price of rice, which had not risen, and the
prices of the manufactured commodities they needed to live. Even
though they were earning far more for the rice they grew since they
had been given back their land under *doi moi*, they couldn't grow
enough to close the gap. (In an example of how the Southerners
set their own rules, Mr. Vy said the official fifteen-year contract
term on return of land didn't apply in Tan Phu, that the land there
had been given back under "permanent contracts.")

All of the children now attended primary school, and the majority continued through the eighth grade in the village's lower secondary school. But just a few families could afford to let their
children complete secondary education at the higher school in the
nearby district town of Cai Lay; a single young man from the
village was attending the university in Can Tho. The poverty was
most eloquent in the Sunday best of three older farmer-veterans of
the battle who posed for a photograph—a short-sleeved shirt and
faded cotton trousers, a homemade safari suit of worn brown cloth,
another homespun safari jacket and mismatching pants.

Twenty-six years before, I had jumped from a helicopter and
walked across the rice fields toward Ap Bac early on the morning
after the battle. As I walked from the council house across those
same rice fields toward the hamlet, I could see again in my mind's
eye smoke rising from the smoldering remnants of houses, the
carcasses of helicopters, the diminutive bodies of ARVN soldiers
stacked along paddy dikes with the toes of their boots pointing up.
Yet when I looked closer on this day I noticed that the coming of
peace was not all that had changed in this landscape. On that
earlier morning many of the rice fields had been bordered by dense
tree lines in the typical pattern of the delta. The lines of trees had

not been an accident. They had been planted by the farmers on the stream banks and on dikes built up like levees along the irrigation ditches and canals because the trees were part of the cycle that sustained life—groves of banana and coconut, orchards of ·other fruit, clumps of bamboo and water palm, and the hardwood trees the peasants grew to pole height for construction. The vegetation around Ap Bac and among the houses within it had also been profuse, every bit of ground put to some use.

The landscape was more open now. The tree lines one could see in the distance were sparse in comparison to their predecessors. Even around the hamlet itself the vegetation was not as dense as it had been. A lot of the irrigation ditches had been restored, but most of the leveelike dikes along them were gone, including the large dike in front of Ap Bac where the Viet Cong had fought from man-deep foxholes concealed under the trees that had flourished there on that long-ago day.

The change helped explain why the land was less productive now, with twice the number of people to feed compounding the problem. The villagers of Tan Phu were still at the beginning of a long process of reconstruction, and perhaps not even they fully remembered what had been lost. The elaborate infrastructure of wet rice culture takes generations of thoughtful labor to build. Twenty-six years earlier there had been no difficulty in flooding the rice lands of Ap Bac and the other hamlets of the village. Then the farmers had been able to keep their paddies flooded all year round through the intricate irrigation system they had created. The battle had occurred at the height of the dry season, and yet the paddies had been full of water.

Although the dike was gone, the villagers had restored the big irrigation ditch in front of Ap Bac. It was full of water, and the footbridge was a single log. Vietnamese country folk traverse one-log bridges handily, but I was leery. I had taken ditchwater baths during the war in tumbles from such rustic acrobat spans. A middle-aged woman in a turban called "No sweat!" in vintage American military slang, dragged up a second log, and threw it across beside the first one to give us better footing. Our good

Samaritan, Mrs. Nguyen Thi Bay, said she had lived in Saigon until 1975, when she had returned to Ap Bac, her native hamlet, to try to earn a livelihood. She was the widow of an ARVN soldier who had been killed during the war. Because her marriage had placed her on the wrong side, she had been given no land and worked as an agricultural laborer for other families. She was cheerful, despite the lot life had dealt her, and put her arm around a nine-year-old girl she said was her daughter.

Ho Chua, an eighty-year-old farmer with a Ho Chi Minh beard, came out of the hamlet carrying a walking staff he didn't seem to need and smoking a cigarette of pungent homegrown tobacco hand-rolled in pink paper. He pointed toward the section of rice paddies just outside of Ap Bac and began telling me how three of the five helicopters had been downed right there. Mr. Chua said he remembered the precise location of the forlorn flying machines because four Americans had taken over his house the day after the battle and used it as living quarters for several days while they tried to repair the aircraft. (Two of the helicopters had been flown out after repair; the third, a hulk, had had to be lifted out by another aircraft.)

I saw three graves a couple of paces behind the spot where Mr. Chua was standing. The graves were looking out over these rice paddies where the Saigon troops and their American advisors had come. The path into the hamlet ran beside the graves, and the children of the hamlet passed them as they walked to and from classes at a new primary school about thirty yards away. Fresh earth, neatly shaped, was heaped up along the length of each grave, and the grass was cut around them. The headstones were plain, of rough, hand-mixed concrete. Etched on each headstone while the concrete had still been wet were the letters "D–C," the Vietnamese abbreviation for "Comrade" *(Dong Chi)*; under these letters a single, identifying name for the man; then "H–S" for "Sacrificed" *(Hy Sinh)*; then the date the man had died: "2–1–63."

The secret Viet Cong account of the battle, captured in an ambush a couple of months afterward in 1963, said that the critical moment had come when Ly Tong Ba's ten-ton armored personnel carriers were about to mount the dike in front of Ap Bac and overwhelm the guerrillas. A squad leader named Dung, the report said, had leapt from the protection of his foxhole, stood on the top of the dike in full view of the machine gunners on the carriers, and thrown a grenade at one of the behemoths. The rest of his squad and other guerrillas along the foxhole line had been inspired by his example. They too had leapt up and hurled grenades, breaking the nerve of Ba's carrier crews with the blast and shrapnel and repulsing the armored machines as the terrified drivers backed away. That night when the Viet Cong regulars withdrew to the safety of their jungle base under the cover of darkness, Squad Leader Dung had not gone with them. He had been killed by an air strike or an artillery barrage after the order had been given to pull back through the hamlet. The report expressed regret that his body could not be retrieved in the darkness to be carried to the battalion base for burial with honor. "Comrade Dung could not come," the Viet Cong account said.

The name etched on the third headstone under the initials for "Comrade" was Dung. I asked Phan Cong Chau, one of the three older farmer-veterans who had assisted the regulars during the battle as hamlet guerrillas—in Chau's case managing to capture two carbines—if he knew anything about the man. Chau said that Dung was the squad leader who had sprung up on the dike to stop the armored carriers with a grenade. He was certain because he had helped to bury all three men after the battle. The two others were members of Dung's squad who had perished with him. "They called his squad the Iron Squad," Mr. Chau said. I had seen the bodies of three Viet Cong when I walked through the hamlet on the morning after the battle. Now I knew what those three men I had seen had done before they died.

When they buried the three guerrillas Mr. Chau and the other farmers had marked the graves. They were thus able to find them when they returned in 1975, he explained. The villagers then poured the concrete and made the headstones. Dung and his two companions were not natives of the village, Mr. Chau said. They

were from two other districts in this province and from the province of Ben Tre across the Tien Giang River, farther south. Their
families had come after the war and wanted to disinter the remains
and rebury them in the men's home villages. Mr. Chau said the
families had been persuaded to leave the three men where they had
fallen. He and the other farmers wanted to show gratitude to these
men who had died for the village, Mr. Chau said, and had promised to tend the graves with care.

On the way back to Saigon I stopped at the building on the
outskirts of the provincial capital of My Tho, where the American
advisors who had fought at Ap Bac had lived. John Vann had been
the commanding officer of the advisory detachment. The place had
been called the Seminary then because in a yet-earlier incarnation
it had been a school for Vietnamese youths studying for the
Roman Catholic priesthood. A sign out front said that it was
currently the Ap Bac Upper Secondary School, reserved for Vietnamese policemen seeking to complete their high school education.

The volleyball court was still in the center of the compound.
The white boundary lines on the tarmac gleamed from a fresh coat
of paint applied by the Vietnamese policemen, who apparently
liked to play the game too. It was late afternoon and the net was
up. I could hear Vann's raspy voice calling, "Come on, let's get
those volleyball teams out there," and the shouts of the American
captains and lieutenants as they played. Those young men had been
my contemporaries, and I had identified with them. They had been
keen officers, the best the U.S. Army had to give, eager for battle,
certain of their cause and their ideals. When we had clambered
aboard the helicopters with the assault troops amidst the racket of
the engines and the whirling dust from the rotor blades we had
thought, "Someday we will triumph, and this will be a better land
for our coming." We had not triumphed, and because of our
coming Vietnam was a wounded land. In the twilight of the
volleyball court I wondered what those young officers would have
thought of the other brave men in the foxholes on the dike had
they known the truth of the war they had been sent to fight.

The buffalos and cattle and goats grazed through the brush among the thousands of graves in the ARVN cemetery off the Bien Hoa Highway not far from Saigon, knocking over a tombstone here and there as they browsed. The place had been meant to be the former Saigon government's equivalent of Arlington National Cemetery. It was begun in the late 1960s, when, under Richard Nixon's "Vietnamization" program to shift the onus of combat to the Saigon forces, the smaller cemeteries could no longer hold the number of dead. In 1972, for example, 39,000 Saigon soldiers died. Altogether, a quarter of a million members of the Saigon forces were killed in action. The coffins were trundled in, but by the time of the debacle in 1975 the laying out of the cemetery itself and the construction of its towering central monument were still unfinished.

A toothless old man in a conical straw hat who was guarding several grazing buffalos said that a couple of people came every day to visit or search for a grave and that at Tet families would cut the brush and clear away the weeds around the burial place of a loved one. There was no one there to visit a grave on the afternoon that Tien and I drove out, just the old man, some boys who were watching other buffalos, cows, and goats, and a group of villagers from a nearby hamlet who were digging up the roads through the cemetery to sell the stones in the roadbeds for house foundations. Some of the graves were tended. The villagers said the families paid them to do it. Other graves were weed-filled holes in the ground because the families had removed the remains for reburial elsewhere.

Chance and the elements were the only attention that most of the graves were getting. Headstones were astray on the ground, jarred loose by the leg of one foraging beast, kicked away by the hoof of another. The ARVN had shrouded the graves of its dead with long cement covers, made like the tops of ancient sarcophagi. Many of these were askew, tilted sideways because the earth underneath had sunk over the years. In one section of the cemetery where the livestock had for some reason not grazed much the brush was so high that it was beginning to hide the burial places.

From the high ground in the middle of the cemetery where the towering concrete skeleton of the unfinished central monument stood, one could look back down the main avenue, lined with eucalyptus trees, and see a pagoda on a hill at the other end. The pagoda had been completed before the finale in 1975. It was a shrine to the dead. The six sets of stairs leading up to it were crumbling. Inside the pagoda was a large memorial tablet, shaped like the stone memorials to feudal mandarins in the ancient Temple of Literature in Hanoi. In front of the tablet was a symbolic grave. "The Land of Your Ancestors Will Always Be Grateful" *(To Quoc Ghi On)*, the words on the tablet read.

The tablet had been defaced. The glazed ceremonial tiles that once covered the symbolic grave before it had been stripped away by scavengers. There was nothing left but brick and mortar. The decorative tiles were also gone from the walls and ceiling of the pagoda, replaced by the obscene graffiti Vietnamese teenagers liked to scrawl.

Squad Leader Dung and his two comrades were cared for by those whose rice fields they won. On the road to Ben Suc was a cemetery where thousands who died on the Communist side in Cu Chi District rested. Brush did not grow amidst their graves. In Washington, the names of each of our Vietnam dead were inscribed on a memorial near the hallowed temple to Abraham Lincoln. No one accepted responsibility for these dead ARVN soldiers. Misguided men in Washington pursuing the fantasies of empire and venal men in Saigon pursuing the lure of power and graft had used them badly in life. In death they were discarded. Tien was saddened by the place. "This should not happen to anyone," he said.